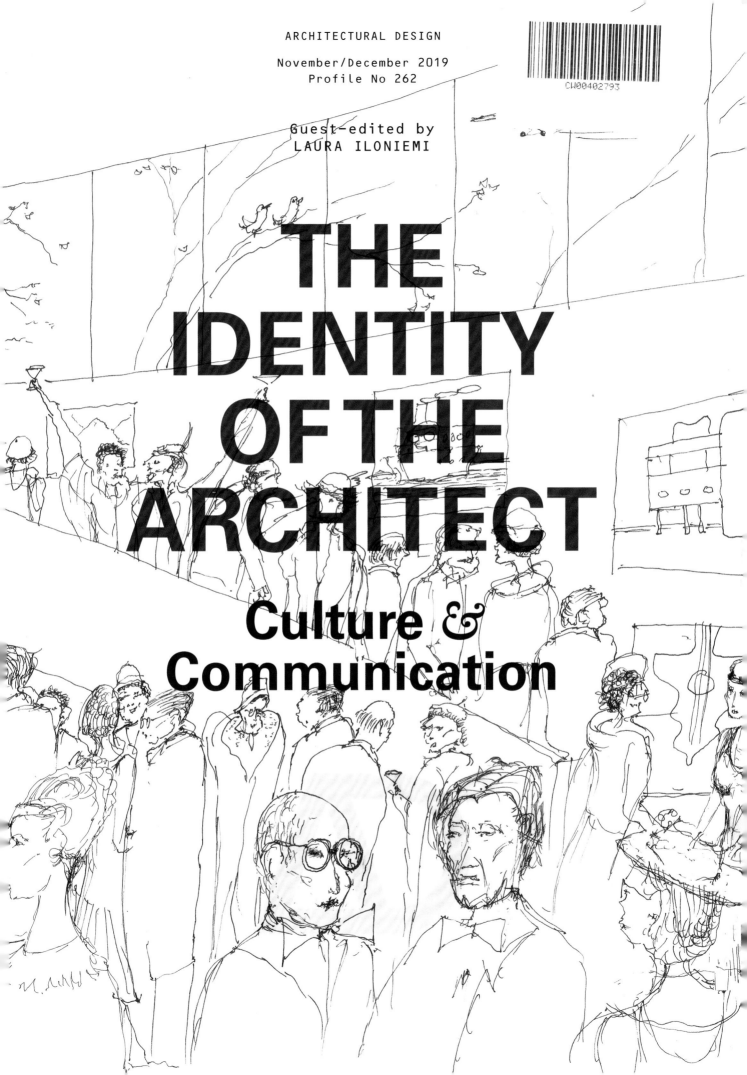

ARCHITECTURAL DESIGN

November/December 2019
Profile No 262

Guest-edited by
LAURA ILONIEMI

# THE IDENTITY OF THE ARCHITECT

## Culture & Communication

Le Corbusier,
Monastery of Sainte-Marie de
La Tourette, Éveux, France,
1960

Paul Rudolph,
Yale Art and Architecture
Building, New Haven,
Connecticut,
1963

2

ISSN 0003-8504
ISBN 978 1119 546214

**Editorial Offices**
John Wiley & Sons
9600 Garsington Road
Oxford
OX4 2DQ

T +44 (0)1865 776868

**Editor**
Neil Spiller

**Commissioning Editor**
Helen Castle

**Managing Editor**
Caroline Ellerby
Caroline Ellerby Publishing

**Freelance Contributing Editor**
Abigail Grater

**Publisher**
Paul Sayer

**Art Direction + Design**
CHK Design:
Christian Küsters
Barbara Nassisi

**Production Editor**
Elizabeth Gongde

**Prepress**
Artmedia, London

**Printed** in Italy by Printer
Trento Srl

**Journal Customer Services**
For ordering information,
claims and any enquiry
concerning your journal
subscription please go to
www.wileycustomerhelp
.com/ask or contact your
nearest office.

**Americas**
E: cs-journals@wiley.com
T: +1 781 388 8598 or
+1 800 835 6770 (toll free
in the USA & Canada)

**Europe, Middle East
and Africa**
E: cs-journals@wiley.com
T: +44 (0)1865 778315

**Asia Pacific**
E: cs-journals@wiley.com
T: +65 6511 8000

**Japan** (for Japanese-
speaking support)
E: cs-japan@wiley.com
T: +65 6511 8010 or 005 316
50 480 (toll-free)

Visit our Online Customer
Help available in 7 languages
at www.wileycustomerhelp
.com/ask

Print ISSN: 0003-8504
Online ISSN: 1554-2769

Prices are for six issues
and include postage and
handling charges. Individual-
rate subscriptions must be
paid by personal cheque or
credit card. Individual-rate
subscriptions may not be
resold or used as library
copies.

All prices are subject to
change without notice.

**Identification Statement**
Periodicals Postage paid
at Rahway, NJ 07065.
Air freight and mailing in
the USA by Mercury Media
Processing, 1850 Elizabeth
Avenue, Suite C, Rahway,
NJ 07065, USA.

**USA Postmaster**
Please send address changes
to *Architectural Design,*
John Wiley & Sons Inc.,
c/o The Sheridan Press,
PO Box 465, Hanover,
PA 17331, USA

**Rights and Permissions**
Requests to the Publisher
should be addressed to:
Permissions Department
John Wiley & Sons Ltd
The Atrium
Southern Gate
Chichester
West Sussex PO19 8SQ
UK

F: +44 (0)1243 770 620
E: Permissions@wiley.com

**Subscribe to** ⚏
⚏ is published bimonthly
and is available to purchase
on both a subscription basis
and as individual volumes
at the following prices.

**Prices**
Individual copies:
£29.99 / US$45.00
Individual issues on
⚏ App for iPad:
£9.99 / US$13.99
Mailing fees for print
may apply

**Annual Subscription Rates**
Student: £90 / US$137
print only
Personal: £136 / US$215
print and iPad access
Institutional: £310 / US$580
print or online
Institutional: £388 / US$725
combined print and online
6-issue subscription on
⚏ App for iPad: £44.99 /
US$64.99

Front cover: © Artwork by
Adam Nathaniel Furman
from '4 Characters in
the 1st Act' furniture
collection, commissioned
by Camp Design Gallery,
Milan, 2017

Inside front cover and
page 1: Purist party,
Maison La Roche-
Jeanneret, Paris.
Drawing by Gabor Gallov

**06/2019**

⚏ ARCHITECTURAL DESIGN

| November/December | Profile No. |
|---|---|
| **2019** | **262** |

Laura Iloniemi's interest in the ways architects define their work began with her MA dissertation on how Alvar Aalto was perceived in the UK. In the Aalto Archives at the architect's studio in Helsinki, it became clear that Aalto had a strategy for gaining international recognition. Iloniemi's continued curiosity as to how modern masters are made led her to pursue a postgraduate degree in museology at the Ecole du Louvre in Paris where she specialised in arts promotion. She returned to Aalto when she wrote a thesis on his approach to both public and private spaces as part of an MPhil degree in architectural history and philosophy at the University of Cambridge.

In the mid-1990s she set up a PR agency seeking to implement principles of communication inspired by studying Aalto's life and work. She has combined these with the curatorial approach to arts promotion advocated by the Ecole du Louvre. While representing Arup over 15 years, she initiated the 'Sustaining Identity' symposia series at the Victoria and Albert Museum in London. At Arup, she also worked with Cecil Balmond and his Advanced Geometry Unit (AGU). In addition to day-to-day public relations, she collaborated with the AGU on the promotion of the Serpentine Gallery pavilions in London, a major exhibition at the Louisiana Museum outside Copenhagen, and a site-specific exhibition at the Graham Foundation in Chicago.

She has also put together campaigns to launch the London offices of Rafael Viñoly Architects and Ushida Findlay, and continues to support architectural practices, established and new, in London and internationally. Together with Make Architects, she has been part of a curatorial team setting up the Architecture Drawing Prize. The co-curators of the annual prize, currently in its third year, are the Sir John Soane's Museum and the World Architecture Festival.

Throughout her time working as a publicist, Iloniemi has reflected, through articles and talks, on how architecture is promoted. Her book *Is It All About Image?* (John Wiley & Sons, 2004) is intended as an individual and non-corporate approach to PR aimed specifically at architects. She has also written for a number of journals. A series for *ArchDaily* observed how a misguided emphasis on indiscriminate coverage or superficial brand values can compromise architectural projects. She has spoken on the subject of identity and public relations as a keynote lecturer at IUAV Venice's 'Image of the Architect – Architect of Image' conference, and at other events including the 'Script' conference in Florence, the Royal Institute of British Architects Leadership Symposium in London, and the World Architecture Festival in Amsterdam. In addition to her work as a publicist, she is currently teaching Part III students at the Architectural Association on the principles of communication and presentation. ⊅

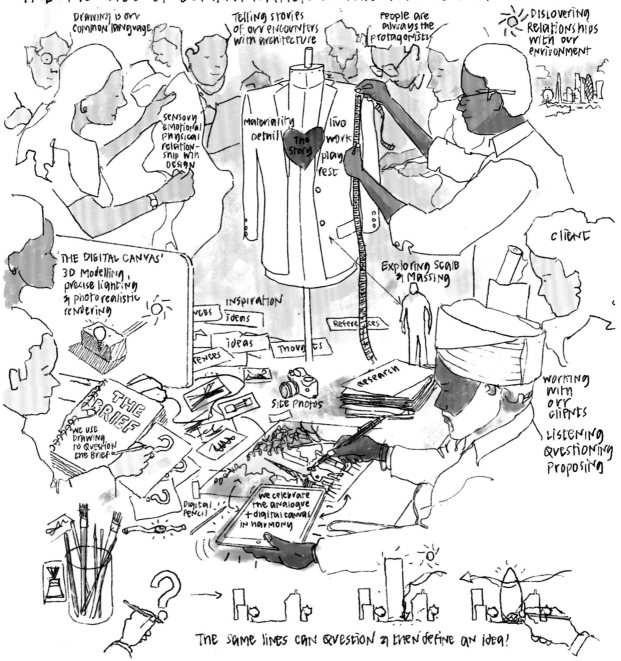

# CREATING WORLDS

## How Identities Are Lost and Found

'Kunstwollen' – in English, 'art will' or 'the willing of art' – is a compelling term to consider when discussing the identity of the architect. It is Alois Riegl's term and its precise definition has challenged art historians, some emphasising purely stylistic and evolutionary thrusts, others notions of artistic urge or intent.[1] At their best, buildings are expressions of architects' beliefs and values, a way of seeing the world and certainly a way of wanting to experience it. The identities of studios that emerge from this sort of practice should be an extension of such a *Kunstwollen*.

Why bother with such an academic conceit? For the simple reason that, today, identity as a concept is muddled with marketing values that have little to do with creative impulses informing the work of practices. Instead, identities or 'brands' seek to fit into the marketplace, to pander to market forces. This has led to a slippery slope where critical discourse and salesmanship become confused, leading some architects to lose their way and, even after decades of practice, to wonder what exactly they stand for. A mid-life crisis, perhaps. An identity crisis, certainly.

### Kunstwollen and Identity
If architects were to consider the culture of their studios and communication more as an expression of their work in the *Kunstwollen* sense rather than conventional management and marketing practices, matters could be different. Consider David Chipperfield, a strong example of an architect who has *willed* the world around him to evoke a particular architectural sensibility. From the studio's internal drawing protocols specifying preferred line-weights to the practice's graphics, to the way projects are photographed and shared with the public, Chipperfield's is a museum-standard performance. This speaks of control and professionalism, but equally of a powerful celebration of the work in the eyes of clients and media alike.

Such worlds resonate with the public's imagination too, because they are seen as poetic confirmation of the very

things these architects' buildings convey. Some may call them 'brands', yet their impact is not achieved through the methods commonly used by branding strategists or 'creatives'. Instead, they are much more aligned with a DIY approach whereby the architect works with carefully selected external graphic designers, photographers and writers while remaining the art director of the process – as David Chipperfield Architects have done. Increasingly, practices have in-house teams able to implement and help provide these skills.

### Branding Bluster
This notion of DIY is described as going 'brandless' by Henrietta Thompson, Editor-at-Large at *Wallpaper\**, in her article 'Is all the sexy signage and marketing mission as necessary as we thought?'.[2] She cites well-known companies that have successfully given up outsourced branding and the price inflation they incur – 'brand tax' – in favour of doing their own thing.

The main challenge with using branding agencies is that they often struggle to promote something that does not fit into our habitual patterns of consumption. Architecture as a discipline and buildings as an art form are simply not within the comfort zone of the service they provide, because architecture by virtue of what it is should have gravitas and its communication should be about an appreciation that gets this across.

David Chipperfield Architects,
Kantine,
Berlin,
2013

The Kantine (left) shares a courtyard with David Chipperfield Architects' Berlin office to the right. Located in Berlin-Mitte, it is open to the public, but is also very much the staff's own canteen. It offers an insight into the world of the studio that reinforces the practice's identity by letting us share in the working environment of its architects.

Narinder Sagoo,
*The Method of Communication is Tailormade for Each Design*,
2019

*opposite:* Drawing, for Foster + Partners, is a common language for both discovery and expression in design. The practice's Art Director, Narinder Sagoo, drew the image on the right for this issue of Ð to show how the act of design and communication are interlinked; so much so that Sagoo describes the practice as both 'communicating design' and 'designing communication'.

Branding, meanwhile, is by no means neutral as an industry. This is clear to anyone familiar with Naomi Klein's seminal book *No Logo* (first published in 1999),[3] which sheds light on the commercialisation of values and beliefs by branding agencies and, in particular, the recent phenomenon of identity politics being used as marketing fodder and derogatorily referred to as 'woke capitalism'.[4] Architects have not been immune to such tendencies rampant in today's communication culture in which anyone and everyone seeks to be an adman by self-branding – a particular trait of the gig economy.

This branding coincides with a time when fear has come into play in terms of survival. Since the early 1990s recession and the subsequent 2008 credit crunch, architects have become ever more aware of the need to sell themselves, and particularly so as their professional status has been compromised by other consultants and contractors increasingly running the show. The fear of not winning work or not having influence has led to a loss of confidence among architects, and perhaps so much so that, in his historical appraisal of the identity of the architect in this issue (pp 14–21), Stephen Bayley argues that it is high time architects reinvent their identities.

**Lost Identities**

Perhaps reinvention is as much about rediscovery as anything else. Recently, architects have been conditioned to downplay the art of what they do and to emphasise assets over aesthetics. In the UK, the government felt a need to create a 'Building Better Building Beautiful' commission to define high-quality design for homes and neighbourhoods. This initiative pointed to an identity crisis in the profession caused by architects' and their institutions' limited ability to get such messages across.

This crisis is due to many architects feeling a deep alienation in terms of what they do. Stephen Parnell summed it up in his 2011 PhD thesis: 'Being an architect was more who I was than what I did.'[5] If architects have this sense of loss, surely there is hope to reignite the very things that have made them want to be architects. Surely there is scope to fight the deadly managerial culture that has crept into the profession, the bland self-important jargon, the mind-numbing CGIs, the lowbrow networking events and even an increasingly corporate comms-style PR. Surely architects can help themselves by thinking of how to celebrate their work imaginatively and so supporting what remains of their craft.

Adam Nathaniel Furman,
*Look Down to Look Up*,
London,
2018

Furman's work, such as this public art commission of five large Ground Art projects for Croydon Council, celebrates the resurgence of ornament and colour in architecture. The wider discourse he has successfully generated on social media and through his writing, for example in his 2017 book *Revisiting Postmodernism* with Sir Terry Farrell, have been hugely energetic and created a revival or movement that supports what his studio does.

This sense of identity crisis has not been helped by an excessive reliance on media coverage to bolster individual practices. Although media exposure is useful in relaying what architects do, the narratives presented through this medium paint only a part of the picture and one that naturally fits within the confines of an editorial team's objectives. Media exposure also often favours the 'star-architect', a phenomenon that is incredibly inward and unhelpful for the profession as a whole. Inward, because virtually no architect is a star in the sense of being a genuine household name. Unhelpful because, as Reinier de Graaf notes in *Four Walls and a Roof* (2017): 'The focus on the importance of individual figures in architecture masks architecture's failing as a collective.'[6]

## Taking Charge

How could architects re-engage collectively? The articles in this issue of *D* address this question from different perspectives while encouraging architects to take back control in making their beliefs resonate in a more convincing and heartfelt way. Some take a critical look as to how communication tools are used, thus helping practices to become more discerning in the way they present their work.

The cover image of the issue, *Pattern from 4 Characters in the 1st Act*, is by Adam Nathaniel Furman whose article (pp 80–87) focuses on how architects use social media as a platform. Architects should see social media as an opportunity to take ownership of the creation of their studios' identities, as Furman himself has done with great aplomb, by sharing his work.

Other articles in the issue are about bringing back a sense of joy. Jonathan Glancey (pp 40–47) discusses this through the example of Le Corbusier and the device of a mask-like persona for the maestro's identity. Gabor Gallov (pp 52–7) writes about the role of drawing in bringing the architect's intent to life, and Robin Monotti Graziadei (pp 58–63) examines through Aldo Rossi's autobiography a humanist predisposition to explaining and describing what architects do.

More critical dimensions as to how architecture has been communicated are present in Juhani Pallasmaa's essay (pp 22–7) challenging the over-emphasis on the way two-dimensional images convey how architecture is experienced. Vicky Richardson (pp 28–33) laments the use of business speak by so many practices and how this has compromised the entire discourse around architecture. Owen Hopkins (pp 68–73) brings a curatorial perspective to the subject of culture and communication in an era of information overload, and Jay Merrick (pp 110–15) tackles the image of architects as these are relayed to him as an architectural critic.

## Around the World

Austin Williams (pp 88–93) and Justine Harvey (pp 94–7) look at identity from the particular geographic perspectives of China and New Zealand respectively. Interestingly, questions of identity are something that art historians from my native Finland are especially well aware of when looking at National Romantic architects. For example, Saarinen Lindgren and Gesellius helped conceive the very idea of Finnish nationhood through their 1900 Finnish Pavilion in Paris and National Museum in Helsinki (1905–10).

Saarinen Lindgren and Gesellius,
National Museum Helsinki,
Finland,
1905-10

The museum was conceived as an exhibition in its own right, referencing different building types. Its entrance hall has ceiling paintings depicting scenes from Finland's national epic, *The Kalevala*. It would be glib to refer to these works of art, or the museum's architecture, as a branding exercise for Finland, yet this sort of confusion between art and marketing is what many branding agencies gladly advocate.

Architects should see social media as an opportunity to take ownership of the creation of their studios' identities

Gabor Gallov,
Drawings of Alvar Aalto's Fortnum & Mason
exhibition in London in 1939, and Aalto
on the boat he acquired in the 1950s,
2019

Aalto won the hearts of international audiences well before he reached similar acclaim in his home country, which led him to name his boat *Nemo propheta in patria*. His furniture, made by Artek, played an important part in disseminating his ideas both in Finland and overseas, as did his own writings and the many publications on his work.

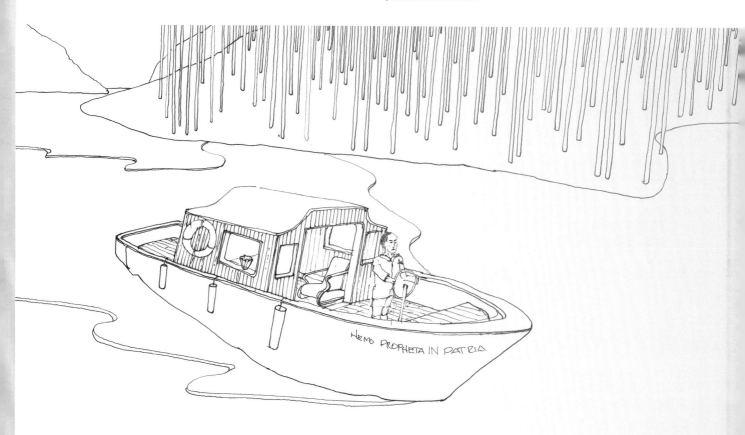

The career which Aalto created for himself during his lifetime was based on his skill to market himself, to find himself the best possible assistants. The myth about Aalto was formed hand in hand with his work

Alvar Aalto's role in later years was also important in creating an embodiment of modern Finnish values. In 1933 he exhibited his work at Fortnum & Mason's department store in London. 'It was not the result of lucky consequence, as one may think,' writes his biographer Göran Schildt.[7] 'The career which Aalto created for himself during his lifetime was based on his skill to market himself, to find himself the best possible assistants. The myth about Aalto was formed hand in hand with his work.'[8] Amongst these assistants, art historian Nils-Gustav Hahl was a key figure, an interpreter and go-to for contacts including the architect's important link to the *Architectural Review*.

In Finland, Aalto is truly a household name. The Finnish 50-euro note features his portrait on one side, and on the other his Finlandia Hall (1971). However, architects in Finland no longer enjoy the status of Aalto and his contemporaries. The erosion of this standing, this vocation, appears, with a few exceptions, to be worldwide today. Concerns relating to the public role of the architect as described by Ian Ritchie in this issue (pp 122–7) will no doubt resonate universally, as will those raised by Caroline Cole (pp 98–103) as she looks at succession in the context of identity. Cole also reflects on the important subject of collaborative identity as a contemporary alternative to the maestro-led one.

The issue also includes examples from practitioners of how they have crafted their identities, ranging from Zaha Hadid Architects' use of product design to convey ideas about the studio's architecture (pp 74–9), to IF_DO discussing their manifesto (pp 116–21), to Jenny E Sabin's academia-led approach (pp 34–9), and BIG's 'worldcrafting' (pp 48–51), which has attained a genuinely global reach. Crispin Kelly (pp 64–7) gives us a client's perspective on identity, a topic that would be interesting to develop in the future in terms of how architects provide their services. Jan Knikker of MVRDV (pp 104–9) touches on this in his piece on the balancing act of communicating with clients versus peers.

Zaha Hadid exhibition,
Palazzo Franchetti,
Venice,
May–November 2016

Seeing Zaha Hadid's paintings at the Palazzo Franchetti was for many a visitor the highlight of the exhibition and of the 15th Venice Architecture Biennale as a whole, making them want to travel to see the studio's buildings around the world.

Lukas Göbl,
*City of Beautiful Bodies*,
2016

The hybrid category winner in the Architecture Drawing Prize 2018 curated by
Make, Sir John Soane's Museum and the World Architecture Festival. The prize
has become an important initiative promoting the role of drawing in advancing
the art of architecture and in communicating the driving concepts behind
designs. Göbl's drawing is about exploring utopia as part of the design process
rather than as a goal in and of itself: an exciting aspect of his practice Göbl
Architektur's future development.

# Identity is as much an internal as external logic for a practice as well as an important, even liberating, support mechanism

## Consistency

The obvious problem in terms of communicating architecture
is that so much of it happens in the absence of being able
to take audiences to the buildings themselves. Photography
plays a huge role in giving us a sense of what these buildings
are about, and talented architectural photographers such as
Hélène Binet and Gareth Gardner, whose photos are featured
in this issue of Ɑ (pp 22–7, 43 and 72–3), give us a great
insight into how we might experience buildings. However,
too little is made of the role of other media, like drawings
and models, to enhance this narrative. Instead, architects'
own websites focus heavily on 'hero shots' of completed
projects. Overall architects have been unimaginative in
adopting digital interfaces and have not made use of the
way in which the Web, for example, supports 3D visuals.
Architectural exhibitions are also predominantly shy in the
way they favour rather dry and inaccessible boards to display
practitioners' work. There are, of course, inspiring exceptions.
A remarkable one was the moving tribute to Zaha Hadid that
her team curated in her memory at the Palazzo Franchetti
during the 2016 Venice Architecture Biennale. The exhibition
was a tantalising way to experience her world even if one
may not have been to a building by Zaha Hadid Architects.
Hadid's paintings in particular were filled with a sense of her
practice's *Kunstwollen*.

By sharing the design process and a studio's thinking
in such an artistic way, architects could elevate the
understanding of what they do. Some have used drawing
skilfully to achieve this, notably Foster + Partners, but
talented, smaller practices too, like London-based architects
Birds Portchmouth Russum or Göbl Architektur in Vienna.

Architects should have their own distinct way to portray their identities. Ones in which they recognise themselves, for identity is as much an internal as external logic for a practice as well as an important, even liberating, support mechanism. The idiosyncrasies of architects' work should thus inform their practices' identities and communicate this with a consistency and flair that help foster a culture for commissioning better architecture. This is about pursuing an aesthetic urge or the same volition that inspires an architect's design process. It is, in fact, about the ability of the architect *to will* an identity around the studio's work. ⌂

**Notes**
1. Svetlana Alpers, 'Style is What You Make It: The Visual Arts Once Again', in Berel Lang (ed), *The Concept of Style*, University of Pennsylvania Press (Philadelphia, PA), 1979, pp 95–118.
2. Henrietta Thompson, 'Is All The Sexy Signage And Marketing Mission As Necessary As We Thought?', *BA Business Life*, November 2017, pp 9–10.
3. Naomi Klein, *No Logo: Taking Aim at the Brand Bullies*, 10th Anniversary Edition, Fourth Estate (London), 2010.
4. Nosheen Iqbal, 'Woke Washing? How Brands Like Gillette Turn Profits by Creating a Conscience', *The Guardian*, 19 January 2019: www.theguardian.com/media/2019/jan/19/gillette-ad-campaign-woke-advertising-salving-consciences.
5. Stephen Parnell, '*Architectural Design* 1954–1972: The Architectural Magazine's Contribution to the Writing of Architectural History', PhD thesis, University of Sheffield School of Architecture, November 2011, p 11.
6. Reinier de Graaf, *Four Walls and a Roof: The Complex Nature of a Simple Profession*, Harvard University Press (Cambridge, MA), 2017, p 16.
7. Göran Schildt, *Inhimillinen Tekijä*, Otava (Helsinki), 1989, p 170.
8. *Ibid.*

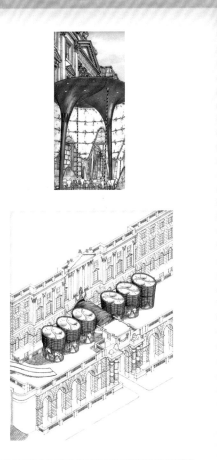

*Somerset House Restaurant, 1999*

Birds Portchmouth Russum,
Somerset House Restaurant competition entry,
London,
1999

Wit is a rare, but all the more captivating quality in architecture. Birds Portchmouth Russum's designs and the studio's exceptionally skilled drawings are often witty or joyous, as in the Somerset House Restaurant triptych here.

# The idiosyncrasies of architects' work should ... inform their practices' identities and communicate this with a consistency and flair that help foster a culture for commissioning better architecture

# RISE, FALL AND REINVENTION

Louis Hellman,
*The Image of the Architect,*
1983

For the *Architects' Journal* of 16 March 1983, a lack of appropriate news items led to a suggestion that the resident cartoonist, Louis Hellman, take as inspiration the newly published book by Andrew Saint: *The Image of the Architect.* The result has proved his most requested cartoon.

**Stephen Bayley**

# THE ARCHITECT'S SHIFTING IDENTITY

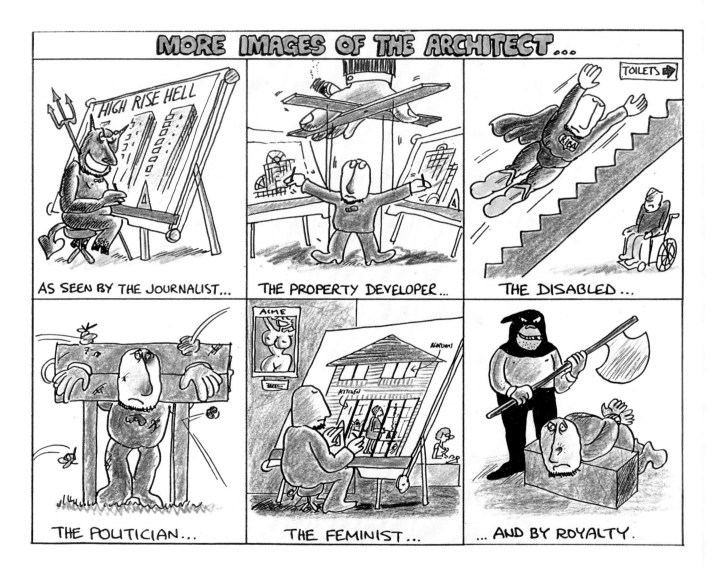

Louis Hellman,
*More Images of the Architect,*
1984

Hellman reprised the *Image of the Architect* idea with *More Images ...*
(*The Architects' Journal*, 5 September 1984) and later with *Even More Images ...,*
*Historic Images ...* and *More Historic Images ... .*

Taking stock of architects' hubris in actuality and fiction, London-based design critic and curator **Stephen Bayley** asks why, recently, the architect has ceased to be a clown or hero in the eyes of popular culture. He posits that the reinvention of the architect is necessary to reclaim this lost prominence, good or bad, in the eyes of the public.

Between 1929 and 1943, the image of the architect underwent a dramatic and amusing change, at least insofar as the literature of the novel was concerned.

Professor Otto Silenus made his first appearance in this country in 1928, on the pages of Evelyn Waugh's *Decline and Fall*.[1] To Waugh, he was a ridiculous figure of fun: a dementedly serious and humourless German architect – almost certainly modelled on Walter Gropius – commissioned by Margot Beste-Chetwynde to design 'something clean and square'. Silenus has attracted his client's attention with his designs for a chewing-gum factory in Hungary, recently published in the architectural press.

Waugh facetiously explains Silenus's design philosophy: 'The problem of architecture as I see it is the problem of art ... the elimination of the human element ... [man] is only happy when a channel for the distribution of mechanical forces.' Soon after her house is built, a horrified Mrs Beste-Chetwynde promptly demolishes it. Waugh's satire characterises Gropius-Silenus as a hopeless incompetent, demented by a useless and impractical vision.

**Clean and Square**

But by 1943 when Ayn Rand published *The Fountainhead*,[2] a different version of 'The Architect' was made popular. Rand's hero is the architect Howard Roark. His curriculum vitae is a tale of heroic posturing, brave independence and absolute refusal to compromise his design principles.

Roark is expelled from architecture school before graduation. Being very butch, he goes to work in a quarry to earn money and build impressive muscles (which he flexes often). Once established in practice, he is taken to court over his eccentric designs for the Stoddard Temple. Later, he is taken to court again when he sets fire to a housing project he has designed because government agents have interfered with the integrity of the original vision. He is a man of action as well as a man of ideas and beliefs. He is an arsonist of ideas.

Evelyn Waugh,
Illustration of Otto Silenus from
*Decline and Fall*,
1928

Evelyn Waugh's sinister Professor Silenus thought the perfect building was a factory because it housed machines, not men. Waugh's satire reveals both the fear and disdain the privileged classes had for ambitious modernists.

Read the internet conversation about Howard Roark and you learn that he is, additionally, either an enigmatic charmer or a sinister dirtbag. What is certain is that he was Ayn Rand's own mouthpiece for her peculiar Objectivist philosophy (a reconciliation of Samuel Smiles's *Self-Help* (1859) and Adolf Hitler's philosophy which detested conformist mediocrity). Before the thrilling winds of first-wave feminism had made such a thing unnecessary, a woman intellectual had to practise such subterfuge, subcontracting outrage to male fictions.

And Rand makes her readers admire Roark because he could maintain dignity and calm even 'under the vibrations of the crowd's enormous collective sneer'. (Rand was obsessed by sex and there are many references to vibrations in her writing.) And Roark describes his philosophy thus: 'I don't make comparisons. I never think of myself in relation to anyone else. I just refuse to measure myself as part of anything. I'm an utter egotist.'

It is generally assumed that Ayn Rand used Frank Lloyd Wright as a model for Howard Roark. Of course, in this matter of the architect's identity, Wright had made his own thrilling and distinctive contribution. With his billowing cape, his cars, his mauve-dyed hair, his unconventional marriages, his taste for argument, his toxic lack of humility and (it is rumoured) his suede underwear, he was a splendid exemplar of Welsh eccentricity.

In his majestic lack of concern for propriety, Wright was a prototype for the popular caricature of the architect as a detestable figure in thrall to his own talent, but contemptuous of the client's needs. Wright's view was that if a roof did not leak, it was simply evidence that the contractor had not been pushed far enough by the designer. In any event, many of Wright's designs were poorly built of shoddy materials, donating to history not just a catalogue of unusual shapes, but also a melancholy inheritance of severe maintenance problems.

Since it was Le Corbusier's belief that 'design is intelligence made visible', a 1962 study of architects' IQs made another contribution to the shifting identity of the profession.[3] This was when Donald Wallace MacKinnon of the University of California, Berkeley's Institute for Personality Assessment discovered that there was a surprisingly non-linear relationship between IQ and 'creativity' (even if IQ is a questionable metric and 'creativity' notoriously difficult to define). Anyway, MacKinnon found that the 'best' designers in architecture school were rarely straight-A students. And he was left wondering whether there was a vast community of excellent untrained architects who were not in practice because they lacked the basic intellectual requirements to enter architecture school in the first place.

Sophia Miroedova,
Illustrations based on *The Fountainhead*,
2015

The works in this personal project by illustrator Sophia Mirodova were inspired by her favourite moments from Ayn Rand's 1943 novel. King Vidor's 1949 film of the book cast Gary Cooper in the role of Howard Roark, an architect nearly demented by egotism. It is thought that Frank Lloyd Wright was the inspiration for the Roark character.

## Why Do Architects Wear Black?

Fashion has more recently made its own distinctive contribution to the identity of the architect. When asked a leading question by a client, the architect Cordula Rau made that question into the title of a book: *Why Do Architects Wear Black?* was published in 2008.[4]

Rau catalogues the answers her fellow professionals gave. It makes a surreal and gloriously revealing read. Existentialism! You can't go wrong with black. And you don't have to change very often. People notice your eyes better and black makes you look more thin. I wear black because life is so sad. Because I am anti-bourgeois. It's tough, yet bohemian, and makes shopping easier since it reduces choice.

Jacques Herzog was flummoxed by the question: 'Nothing occurs to me really. Probably because so many architects wear it.' So here is Herzog as an uninspired conformist. Peter Eisenman demonstrated the stylish cosmopolitanism for which the New York Five were known when he answered Rau: 'I don't wear schwartz.' But most telling of all was Wolf D Prix of Coop Himmelb(l)au. Architects wear black, he said, because 'they fear for their future'.

Since Almighty God has been described as 'the Great Architect of the Universe', mortal architects rarely feel an inclination towards patience or humility. Indeed, the intemperate bragging of neo-divine authority is the tone of voice architects have often employed even before Howard Roark: 'Architecture aims at Eternity' according to Christopher Wren.[5] No sense of understatement there.

Yet while God is not fallible, architects usually are. The history of recriminations about architects began in 1767 when Teofilo Gallacini published his *Trattato sopra gli errori degli architetti*. And his most remarkable successor was the greatest French novelist.

A defining work of 19th-century literature, absurd and knowing simultaneously, is Gustave Flaubert's *Dictionnaire des idées reçues*.[6] Published as a supplement of his unfinished novel *Bouvard and Pécuchet* (1881), this is a satirical catalogue of platitudes, a guide to common opinion. Whether Flaubert himself ever agreed with what he wrote remains deliciously uncertain.

My favourite entry concerns architects. Flaubert writes that they 'are all imbeciles, always building staircases in the wrong place'. Obviously an overstatement, it nonetheless reveals an eternal truth: most people are unhappy with the buildings they occupy. And they blame the designer. The relationship between architect and client is almost always doomed: the crazy ambition of the one is almost always at odds with the cruel parsimony or even material needs of the other. And how rarely architectural visions survive the scrutiny of real-world use, viz: Professor Silenus and Frank Lloyd Wright.

## What Is An Architect?

Simple questions being best, what is an architect?

What we now call the 'professions' were in the Middle Ages the province of the clergy – a 'profession' being an occupation requiring a skilled intellectual technique. And it was from the Church that the first universities evolved. And these newly emerging professions gathered themselves into associations to guarantee the competence and integrity of their members' work.

For those seeking background to the status anxieties felt by many professional architects, a very short history of professional associations in Britain is useful evidence. Lawyers became the first profession when the Inns of Court were founded in the 15th century; doctors followed in 1518 with the foundation of the Royal College of Physicians; apothecaries became a profession in 1617; and the Law Society was founded in 1739. In 1745 the Company of Surgeons professionalised the sawbones' craft, and animal medicine was recognised as professional in 1791 with the creation of the Royal Veterinary College.

WHY DO
ARCHITECTS
WEAR
BLACK?

BIRKHÄUSER

Cordula Rau,
*Why Do Architects Wear Black?,*
2008

Cordula Rau is a German architect who worked on BMW Welt in Munich, the car-maker's huge vanity project. Her 2008 book mischievously asked (and answered) an important question about the architect's identity.

Narinder Sagoo,
2019

Sagoo, a specialist in architectural visualisation, is an art director at Foster + Partners in London. He has adapted the Sikh headdress, tassel loafers, jeans, cardigan and polo shirt to the black uniform of his profession.

The architects had to wait until 1834 when the Institute of British Architects was founded, 16 years after the creation of the Institute of Civil Engineers. Only dentists are younger, professionally speaking, than architects although they are inclined to wear white rather than black.

Of course, building designers existed before architecture was institutionalised in 1834, but there was a tendency to suggest that art as much as science was a part of the calling. For example, perhaps the very first reference to 'architect' in English occurs in John Shute's *The First and Chief Groundes of Architecture*, published in 1563.[7] He describes himself as a 'Paynter and Archytecte'. Fifty years later, Inigo Jones designed the Queen's House in Greenwich. Before he was appointed Surveyor of the King's Works in 1615, he had been a painter and a designer of theatrical masques. This, it seems, was adequate preparation for becoming an architect.

Am I an artist who understands bricks and mortar, cantilevers and rebar, a visionary whose magnificent concepts are sensibly moderated by my nice understanding of building techniques? Or am I a reliable technician distinguished by an element of aesthetic sensibility? A builder with taste? Or an artist with common sense?

These questions of self-image, still not wholly resolved, are perhaps the most telling aspect of the early modern architects' identity. Thus, the motion 'Architecture: A Profession or an Art?' constituted a momentous debate organised by and animating the by then Royal Institute of British Architects in 1891. The grounded opinion was that a proper profession could not possibly be 'artistic' and that anyone inclined to follow the irregular habits and practices of the artist would be unlikely to qualify as a 'professional'. Wounded by this distinction, Richard Norman Shaw wrote an essay somewhat apologetically called 'That an Artist is Not Necessarily Impractical'.[8]

In a different form, that debate remains active today. Architects have been de-skilled. Once you could say that an architect's job was to survey land, devise plans, estimate costs, make drawings, supervise construction, manage contracts and administer a snagging list throughout the defects liability period. But now most of those tasks have become the professional responsibility of others. 'What exactly are architects for?' is a question whose simplicity is deceptive.

Jean Nouvel, ENIGME A TICS gaming table for Bottega Ghianda, 2018 and OXYMORE chair for Figueras, 2012

Jean Nouvel is the leading French entrant in the global architectural celebrity challenge. He has recognised that fame brings cash value to his 'brand' which now extends beyond mere buildings to furniture and wallpaper, marketed by established furnishing and lighting brands such as NEMO, Bottega Ghianda and Figueras.

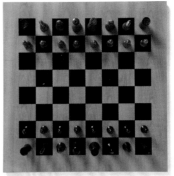
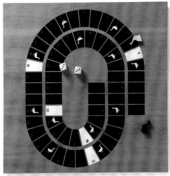

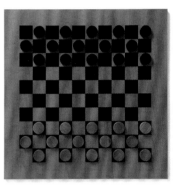

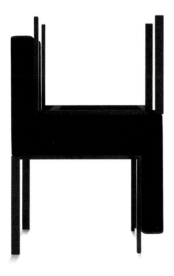

# Time soon, I think, for a reinvention of the architect's identity since, on the whole, people do not much care for the architectural profession

## Tragic Voodoo

One answer is that architects are all for becoming brands. Although this applies most aptly to successful winners of well-reported international competitions than it does to a specialist in side-returns in Balham.

With success in competitions comes media exposure. And with that exposure comes familiarity. And with that familiarity comes desire. I mean a desire from clients to consume an architectural brand as if it were luxury goods from LVMH or Kering.

Structural engineers, CAD visualisers, HVAC consultants, interior designers, landscapers, quantity surveyors, geophysicists, contractors and marketing experts now make sure an original design is realised, leaving the architect to become perhaps an artist, but certainly a brand.

The evolution of brands has tracked the history of modern business. And now it is tracking architecture. Once the product itself was essential, now the image has exceeded it in value.

Victoria Beckham, no engineer, is a creative consultant to Land Rover. FC Barcelona sees *fútbol* only as the origin of its business activities. It now sells branded wine. Jean Nouvel sells branded designs.

So, in this argument, the architect is both a greater and a lesser creature than heretofore. Lesser because his or her practical contribution to the building is perhaps smaller than it has ever been in history. Greater, because that same architect is now selling a global brand with a *pistonnage*.

Friedrich Nietzsche knew that all of life is a question of taste. And if he were alive today, he would say all of life is about branding, or identity. Architects have always wanted to project the spirit of the age. And that is exactly what they do when they become brands. Tragic voodoo? Maybe it is.

Therefore, some of us still yearn for the touching, tangible certainties of dear Professor Silenus. Brands may be promises, but promises are easily broken. Time soon, I think, for a reinvention of the architect's identity since, on the whole, people do not much care for the architectural profession.

It is a very long time since anyone bothered making an architect the subject of a novel, a fiction, a fable or a film. A very long time since architects appeared either clowns or heroes. And that is sadly eloquent. ᗄ

### Notes

1. Evelyn Waugh, *Decline and Fall*, Chapman and Hall (London), 1928.
2. Ayn Rand, *The Fountainhead*, Bobbs-Merrill Company (Indianapolis, IN), 1943.
3. Donald W MacKinnon, 'The Identification of Creativity', *Applied Psychology*, 12 (1), January 1963, pp 25–47: https://onlinelibrary.wiley.com/doi/abs/10.1111/j.1464-0597.1963.tb00463.x.
4. Cordula Rau, *Why Do Architects Wear Black?*, Springer (Vienna and New York), 2008.
5. Christopher Wren, 'Of Architecture', in *Parentalia; or Memoirs of the Family of the Wrens* [1750, compiled by his son Christopher], Gregg Press (Farnborough), 1965, Appendix, p 351.
6. For English translations of selections from Flaubert's *Dictionnaire des idées reçues*, see Stephen Bayley, *A Dictionary of Idiocy*, Gibson Square Books (London), 2003.
7. John Shute, *The First and Chief Groundes of Architecture* [1563], facsimile edition, Country Life (London), 1912: https://archive.org/details/firstchiefground00shut/page/n8.
8. Richard Norman Shaw, 'That an Artist is Not Necessarily Impractical', in R Norman Shaw and TG Jackson (eds), Architecture: *A Profession or an Art*, John Murray (London), 1892, pp 1–15.

# Design for Sensory Reality

## From Visuality to Existential Experience

Purely ocular-centric perception is still dominant in architectural creation. Decrying the narrowness of this approach, Finnish architect, writer and educator **Juhani Pallasmaa** argues for a more holistic appreciation of architecture as a way of communicating the power and embodied experience of the built environment through all the body's senses.

Peter Zumthor,
Therme Vals,
Vals,
Switzerland,
1996

Like all the other images accompanying this article, this photograph is by Hélène Binet. Her photographs are true documentations of buildings, but they depict the sensory and mental experience, rather than physical reality. They are examples of empathic architectural photography that turns into a multisensory and poetic presence. While mediating perceptual subtleties of architecture, they are autonomous works of photographic art.

Architecture has been regarded, theorised, taught and practised primarily as a visual discipline, and consequently, environments and buildings are developed through visual images, means and representations. However, regardless of the historical dominance of vision, architecture is essentially an art form of all the senses in interaction. Our experiential sense of reality calls for the interplay of the senses. Fused into a unified experience, these sensations give rise to a multisensory experience of reality. 'My perception is not a sum of visual, tactile and audible givens: I perceive in a total way with my whole being: I grasp a unique structure of the thing, a unique way of being, which speaks to all my senses at once,' Maurice Merleau-Ponty observes.[1] Only this fully integrated experience can project the veracity of the real.

### Sensory Multiplicity

It is evident that the visually perceived aspects of design are developed and communicated through visual means. But how do we conceive the auditory, haptic, olfactory or taste qualities of the building in our imagination, or the peripherally experienced atmospheres and feelings of settings? We have taken the primacy of vision as given in architecture, but there is evidence that man's earliest spaces were conceived or selected for sound and acoustic effects rather than visual qualities. Cultural historians also testify that until the 17th century the most important senses in human environmental experience were hearing and smell, and vision came far behind these primary senses.[2]

Even in visual perception there is an ideated haptic experience that informs us of materiality, hardness, surface texture, weight and temperature. This tactile experience integrated in vision was called *modénature* by Le Corbusier in his 1923 manifesto of modern architecture, *Vers une architecture* (commonly translated as *Towards a New Architecture*).[3] Gaston Bachelard, the philosopher of science and poetic imagery, divided images into two categories – formal and material – and he argued that the latter type convey deeper emotional experiences.[4] The haptic qualities concealed in visual perceptions have a crucial role in the feel of the architectural design. The frequent uninvitingness and hardness of contemporary architecture seems to arise largely from the rejection of this hidden hapticity. We touch, hear, smell and taste through vision in addition to our specialised senses. Besides, as designers we are taught to be aware of only focused vision, but unfocused peripheral perceptions seem to have a more important role in our experience of spatial qualities, situations, atmospheres and feelings. How, then, does the designer concretise these multiple and often vague experiences in his or her working process and how are they communicated to the craftsmen and builders? In fact, the experiential reality of a meaningful piece of architecture is not only the sum of its sensory properties, as it generates its own existential world, which we interact with through our sense of self and consciousness. 'In a word, the [artistic] image is not a certain meaning expressed by the director but an entire world reflected as in a drop of water,' Andrei Tarkovsky, the poet of cinematic experiences, argues.[5] Memorable architectural entities are similarly also entire unique worlds.

# The haptic qualities concealed in visual perceptions have a crucial role in the feel of the architectural design

Peter Zumthor,
Bruder Klaus Field
Chapel, Mechernich,
Germany,
2007

## Designing for the Neglected Senses

Sounds and acoustic qualities are usually consciously and methodically dealt with only in the design of concert halls, auditoria and churches, but every built room and outdoor space has its specific aural qualities. During the past two decades, sonic environments and soundscapes have become the subject of study for musicians, sound artists, psychologists and dancers, but regrettably less for architects. Some of the recent international conferences on sonic environments have included soundwalks – excursions through ordinary urban, industrial and park environments focusing on the multitude of sounds, natural or generated by man, and their emotional meanings, both pleasurable and disturbing. The participants are usually surprised at the richness of ordinary soundscapes, as we do not normally notice it. We push it to the background in our conscious observation. How can an architect sense the sonic ambience of the design and communicate these intentions? How do sonic qualities become conscious objectives in the design process which includes participants with differing professional backgrounds?

Most of us would probably consider smells and tastes the least meaningful sensations in architecture. Yet, the smell of burned candles and incense of centuries gives an identifiable and memorable character to an old cathedral, and even the nearly subliminal odours of stone, brick, lime, concrete and wood materials, of which the space is built, contribute to the emotional atmosphere and sense of place and reality. Every home has its unique odour, and biologists even suggest that we unconsciously select our mate through odour. Smells are everywhere and they give identities to our experiences. Even professions are identifiable with specific odours – just think of the smell of a cabinetmaker's, shoemaker's, blacksmith's or printer's workshop, or the studios of various artists. We recognise the specific smells of railway stations, libraries, department stores, market halls and sports facilities, but how can we articulate and specify the odours of the spaces we are designing?

Most architects would probably deny the role of tastes in their design work. Yet tastes and smells interact, and most materials – especially natural ones, such as various kinds of stone, wood, metal and textile – give rise to subliminal sensations of smell and taste. Colourful and polished marbles invoke experiences of taste, and even the desire to touch the surfaces with one's tongue. Our first contact with the world in early infancy takes place through the mouth; psychoanalytical literature calls this internalisation of the world through the mouth 'introjection'. Are there ways of utilising smells and tastes as conscious qualities of architectural design?

## Designing Experience

Design takes place through visual media and communication, but during the past couple of decades the experiential and phenomenological interest has gained ground to challenge design that is based solely on visual composition, geometry and formal aspirations. An interest in architectural ambiences and atmospheres has emerged and widened the understanding of the scope of architectural experiences and impacts beyond focused percepts. The sense of scale and proportion alone can evoke specific ambiences, both appealing and irritating. These new interests and sensibilities

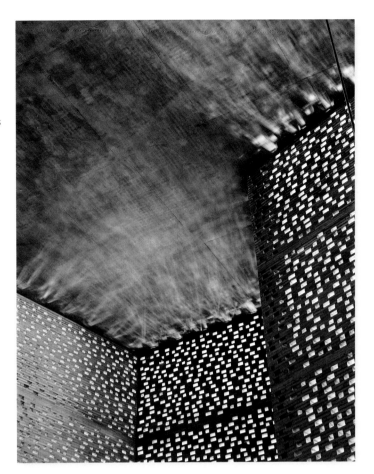

Peter Zumthor,
Kolumba Museum,
Cologne,
Germany,
2007

Le Corbusier,
Monastery of Sainte-Marie de La Tourette,
Éveux,
France,
1960

suggest novel perceptions and design methods, such as the use of 'scores' and literary means for the purposes of concretising and articulating layered, multisensory, dynamic experiences and temporal sequences, such as a walk through a park or a shopping street. The art form of dance has developed ways of choreographing the temporal continuum of movements, and new music has introduced ways of scoring complex musical entities beyond traditional notation. Architecture is similarly a choreography of movements, actions, experiences and emotions. Garden and landscape design are engaged in processes of gradual change and growth, such as the changing aesthetic effects of flowers and plants. The traditional techniques of architectural presentation depict static forms, not dynamic situations and processes of becoming and change. The notion of scores was introduced in the context of architecture in the 1960s by the American landscape architect Lawrence Halprin in his projects ranging from shopping streets to landscapes, parks and fountains.[6]

Along with the phenomenological and experiential interests in architecture and environments, new means of concretising and mediating sensory and expressive realities have also emerged, especially through literary and poetic suggestion. When reading a fine literary text, we imagine complex environmental entities, spaces, buildings, human situations and characters, on the basis of the author's verbal suggestions. This magical capacity of the poet's or novelist's word could well expand the planner's and architect's spatial, situational and material imagination. In their Amangiri Resort hotel project in Kane County, Utah (2008), Marwan

Al-Sayed, Wendell Burnette and Rick Joy consciously focused on the fused and true experiential qualities through literary description, instead of showing the features of the visual design through drawings.[7] A recent study in the use of verbal and literary means in urban design is Klaske Havik's book *Urban Literacy: Reading and Writing Architecture* (2014).[8] 'Writing architecture' is now turning into a valid concept.

**The Biological Dimension**

In addition to the five Aristotelian senses, we have sensory systems that we have not consciously recognised or utilised in architecture. The philosophy of Rudolf Steiner categorises 12 senses – touch, life sense, self-movement sense, balance, smell, taste, vision, temperature sense, hearing, language sense, conceptual sense and ego sense.[9] The most important one in architectural experience could well be the existential sense (the Steinerian life sense and ego sense combined). We respond to architecture through our entire sense of being rather than vision in isolation. How does an architect imagine, conceptualise and communicate experiences evoked by the existential sense? To complicate the question of the senses and concretise their impacts, we have biologically determined mechanisms, such as unconsciously manipulated spatial distances in different behavioural situations, which the anthropologist Edward T Hall revealed in his seminal books during the 1960s and 1970s.[10] He also showed the culture-specific roles and hierarchies of the senses, and these anthropological facts question the ethical ground of design activities across cultural boundaries. Design in an alien cultural context necessarily implies the danger of misinterpretation and oversimplification of subliminal behavioural codes and the neglect of sensory realities alien to the differing cultural backgrounds of designers. In the field of architecture the uncritically accepted processes of globalisation are also fundamentally disputable. Hall further pointed out that research had revealed that even our endocrine glands communicate with the outside world and with other humans.[11] The latest expansion in the understanding of how we are interacting with the world is research on our intestinal bacteria, which process vital information and reactions of our metabolisms in relation to our life situation. What are the consequences of the fact that we have more bacterial DNA than human DNA, on our understanding of environmental design?

It is beyond doubt that the architect's task calls for an understanding of phenomena beyond vision, and subtleties of interaction that can hardly be communicated through visual means. The seminal requirement in today's research, education and practice is to expand the designer's imaginative and empathic capacities beyond the visual realm into an embodied, empathic and immersive identification and understanding. This understanding can be achieved through empathic internalisation and imagination. Our senses and behaviour are fundamentally biologically conditioned, and architectural education should also include aspects of biology. The veracity of our experienced reality is in its layered, orchestrated and interactive essence, which engages us as complete human beings with all our senses, emotions, instincts, memories and imagination.

Dimitris Pikionis,
Landscaping around the Acropolis,
Athens,
Greece,
1957

Traditional Chinese Garden,
Suzhou,
China

These questions call for a biological and bio-historical understanding of ourselves, and that understanding may eventually answer the questions that have been posed above. 'Our greatest problem arises from the fact that we do not know what we are, and do not agree on what we want to become', Edward O Wilson – the biologist and spokesman of biophilia, 'the science and ethics of life' – argues thought-provokingly.[12] Design also needs to be grounded in a biologically informed understanding. ᴆ

**Notes**
1. Maurice Merleau-Ponty, 'The Film and the New Psychology', in *The Visible and the Invisible*, Northwestern University Press (Evanston, IL), 1968, p 48.
2. See, for instance, Robert Mandrou as quoted in Jay Martin, *Downcast Eyes: The Denigration of Vision in Twentieth-Century French Thought*, California University Press (Berkeley and Los Angeles), 1994, pp 34–5.
3. Le Corbusier, *Towards a New Architecture*, The Architectural Press (London), 1959.
4. Gaston Bachelard, *Water and Dreams: An Essay on the Imagination of Matter*, The Pegasus Foundation (Dallas, TX), 1983, p 1.
5. Andrei Tarkovsky, *Sculpting in Time: Reflections on the Cinema*, Bodley Head (London), 1986, p 110.
6. See Lawrence Halprin, *The RSVP Cycles: Creative Processes in the Human Environment*, George Braziller (New York), 1970, and *Process: Architecture 4*, February 1978.
7. See Juhani Pallasmaa, *Rick Joy: Desert Works*, Princeton University Press (New York), 2002, p 20.
8. Klaske Havik, *Urban Literacy: Reading and Writing Architecture*, nai010 (Delft), 2014.
9. See Albert Soesman, *Our Twelve Senses: Wellsprings of the Soul*, Hawthorn Press (Stroud, Gloucestershire), 1998.
10. See Edward T Hall, *The Hidden Dimension*, Anchor Books, Doubleday (New York), 1966, and Edward T Hall, *Beyond Culture*, Anchor Books (New York), 1976.
11. The research on the chemical communication of the endocrine glands was carried out by AS Parkes and HM Bruce in 1961: *The Hidden Dimension, op cit*, pp 33–4.
12. Edward O Wilson, *Biophilia: The Human Bond With Other Species*, Harvard University Press (Cambridge, MA and London), 1984, p 20.

# The architect's task calls for an understanding of phenomena beyond vision, and subtleties of interaction that can hardly be communicated through visual means

Sigurd Lewerentz,
Church of St Mark,
Björkhagen, Sweden,
1960

**Vicky Richardson**

# SLIPPERY WHEN WET

## THE CORPORATE LANGUAGE OF ARCHITECTURE

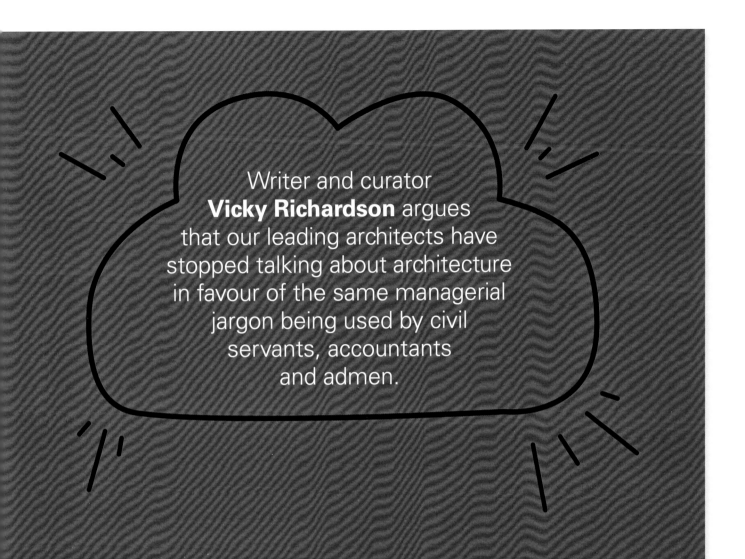

Writer and curator **Vicky Richardson** argues that our leading architects have stopped talking about architecture in favour of the same managerial jargon being used by civil servants, accountants and admen.

Architects are notorious for obscuring their work with words: notions about a sequence of spaces or the legibility of plans can make it difficult for lay people to penetrate the discourse. It is often said that architects just can't write. Counterposing the mindset of a designer to that of a writer is a well-established idea. In *Words and Buildings* (2000), the definitive study of architecture and writing, Adrian Forty explains the fashionable Modernist idea that every art form offers a unique experience that cannot be replicated in another medium. Or to put it more directly, 'Build – don't talk', as Forty quotes Mies van der Rohe.[1]

Despite the implicit idea that language could not get close to describing architecture, Modernist critics and architects introduced their own coded language that still dominates thinking and writing today. Words such as 'space', 'volume', 'design' and 'structure', according to Forty, made buildings and places that are concrete, abstract.[2] In the late 1960s the 'linguistic turn' in philosophy accentuated the tendency towards obscure architectural language as Postmodernism came to dominate the teaching of history and theory in schools of architecture. With architectural writing established as a form of architectural practice in itself, the over-theorisation of architecture reinforced the impression of architects as aloof elitists.

Today though, a very different tendency is threatening architecture, as abstract, theoretical language is increasingly being replaced by the jargon of business management in which 'architecture' is rarely mentioned at all and instead 'holistic solutions are delivered by passionate teams'.

A brief analysis of the words and phrases used by the UK's top-10 architects in the AJ100 survey (2018)[3] shows a predominance of phrases such as 'delivering projects', 'bespoke strategies' and 'collaborative team-working'. Such terms ooze from the 'about us' sections of websites and marketing brochures. The more ordinary the architecture, the more 'passionate and committed' are the 'talented, multidisciplinary teams'.

The danger of this new corporate language is that it does little to illuminate architects' ideas or to clarify the relationship between design and society. Writing, as Forty argues, is a fundamental part of the practice of architecture – as important as photography or drawing.[4] Language is essential in the design and communication of buildings. Articulating architectural ideas in words – whether spoken or written – allows architects to be reflexive, to explain their intentions, to persuade clients and to share ideas with their peers and wider audiences.

### Why Architects Write

Much has been written about architectural criticism, but writing by architects about their own work is discussed less often even though it has an important influence on the press and broader ideas about architecture. In the past, such writing has been motivated by the desire of architects to articulate and explain their ideas to their peers, related professionals and clients. Rather than bashing the profession for elitism or criticising architects for not being able to write, it is worth asking why today's architectural language has become so drained of meaning and seemingly influenced by corporate thinking, and to consider the effect of this on practice itself.

Many architects consciously avoid writing about their work, and obeying Mies's instruction prefer to allow their buildings to speak for themselves. However, in a critical discipline that constantly struggles to define itself and draw boundaries with related practices such as building, sculpture, engineering and art, articulating judgement and intention is a vital part of architectural practice.

In her essay 'Words about Architecture' (2009), Denise Scott Brown reflects on the way architecture and writing are closely linked in her work with Robert Venturi: 'Bob and I write mainly to clarify our ideas,' she says. 'As makers and doers, we have evolved a troika between looking/learning, writing/theorising and designing/building.'[5] Writing itself varies according to its function, says Scott Brown, whether the 'expository texts' of professional life, the everyday prose, or the 'belles-lettres' required for descriptions of buildings. She points out that a client's brief is also a verbal statement, which raises the same problem architects face of 'creating the physical from the verbal'.

## A New Type of Jargon

One explanation for the increasing use of corporate language in architecture is that the profession is mimicking the way clients speak. Perhaps the all-pervasive practice of writing bids has resulted in architects simply reflecting the values and business culture of developers and public clients.

A striking feature of the new writing is that it discusses 'approach' and 'studio culture' rather than the built outcome. So, for example, many of the UK's leading practices are at pains to point out that they listen to clients and respond to the specific conditions of the brief, rather than imposing predetermined ideas. They explain that they work with integrity, responsibility and a commitment to society and the environment.

But despite the claims that their approach differentiates the practice, virtually identical declarations appear on the websites of most of the leading British architects and construction industry consultants. For example, UK-based international design practice Scott Brownrigg says that what makes its approach different is a 'sense of responsibility to the world and to the industry ... To leave the world better than we found it.'[6]

Few practices discuss themselves as architects specifically, and are more likely to use terms such as 'designer' or 'industry professional'; they fall over themselves to be seen as strategists or members of the construction team, eager to collaborate, listen and engage with fellow consultants, clients, users and, of course, 'stakeholders'.

It is not just so-called 'commercial architects' that are guilty of using management jargon. Influential emerging practices such as Architecture 00 and Assemble, pepper their profiles with similar words and phrases, describing themselves as 'innovative' and 'award-winning' along with virtually every other practice.

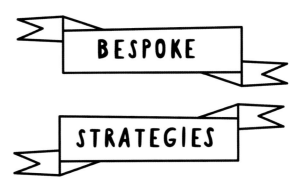

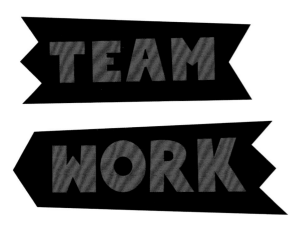

## Uniformly Different

Architectural management jargon whitewashes the distinctive approach or style of practices that were traditionally led by strong individuals – for example Grimshaw and Allies and Morrison – and makes them sound identical to companies such as Atkins or Scott Brownrigg, which are commercially successful but have no signature. Indeed, if you swapped the text between any of these firms no one would notice. So, while architects seek to point out what distinguishes them from their competitors, the new managerial language creates an amazing consistency between them. The eccentricity and distinctiveness of architects such as Sir John Soane, Ernö Goldfinger or Sir Edwin Lutyens is very much a thing of the past.

Few of our leading architects explain their work as part of a tradition of architecture, whether in terms of style, influence, material or formal qualities. Instead they downplay distinctive ideas in order to come across as collaborative. 'We are part of a team,' stresses one; while another 'actively seeks collaboration and works closely with others to learn new skills'. Foster + Partners 'encourages innovation and collaboration', and its 'diverse workforce' shares a 'passion' for design,[7] while BDP delivers 'innovation through collaboration'.[8]

The emphasis is on listening and communicating: 'the architect is a communicator, and design is about listening and bringing together ideas, then guiding and coordinating the team,' says Hawkins\Brown,[9] while Sheppard Robson says it has an 'openness and agility that engages with our clients' specific requirements and aspirations'.[10]

## Openness and Agility

Understanding the clients and users of buildings, which was fundamental to Modernist ideas about function and programme, has little to do with today's 'listening', which shies away from critically engaging with a brief. Architects' reluctance to speak about their specific contribution reflects a defensive stance and a notion that commercial success comes from a lack of specificity about skills and experience.

The art of marketing, it seems, is to offer bespoke solutions at the same time as doing everything. In fact many practices have dropped the word 'architecture' altogether and prefer to speak about 'developing strategies for the built environment' or 'making places', while the service they offer is 'integrated' and 'multidisciplinary', often involving sociologists, anthropologists and artists, as well as architects. In its attempt to cover all bases, one leading practice ends up with the clumsy phrase, 'we design very different buildings for very different people to use in very different ways'.

## Values and Added Value

The final and perhaps most important aspect of the new managerial language is the statement of company values. The idea of having core values or a vision statement is ubiquitous in business, having originated in America, and been made popular by the advertising industry. US business magazine *Forbes* says that mission statements are a key way for companies to differentiate themselves in the market.[11] The irony is that – as in business – many architects' statements of values are identical to one another and there is very little attempt to explain how they relate to the buildings and places they have designed.

Today most practices claim their work is driven by a philosophy or set of values that lies outside the discipline of architecture. Often this is about improving the planet or the lives of people, whether their aim is to 'transform communities' (Grimshaw),[12] 'foster community' (Allies and Morrison),[13] or 'contribute to the social, environment and economic health of our communities' (Atkins).[14]

Adrian Forty points out that architects have long referred to society as a means to describe their work. In the 19th and early 20th centuries, he writes, they tended to locate the 'social' quality of architecture in its production, for example by arguing that architecture's potential to liberate society lay in its ability to take advantage of new techniques of production.[15] Later, says Forty, architects such as Christopher Alexander were dedicated to finding architectural expression for social forms, or, as with Herman Hertzberger, used language in a particular way to articulate an idea about the relationship between society and architecture.[16] Today, by contrast, the UK's leading practices reference community and the social as means of expressing values or as corporate positioning, rather than as a method of explaining the precise way in which their designs relate to society.

In line with the wider attempt to measure the economic value of design and the arts, the curator of the 2016 Venice Architecture Biennale, Alejandro Aravena, played a key role in reinforcing the social justification for architecture. Announcing the Biennale theme, he wrote:

> We are interested in how architecture can introduce a broader notion of gain: design as added value instead of an extra cost; architecture as a shortcut towards equality. We want to see cases where architecture did, is, and will make a difference in winning those battles and expanding those frontiers.[17]

Aravena's call to discuss architecture in terms of its social impact is now all-pervasive; and despite his criticism of the 'property developers who use buildings to chase huge profits', his values and value-led approach to architecture sit very comfortably in the corporate world. Unfortunately, the increasing references to community, society and the good of the planet in architecture have not led to a more in-depth enquiry into the specific ways that design addresses social need or relates to it.

## Legal Latitude

The uniformity of architects' statements must make us suspicious about the truth of what is being written, and question the extent to which their words tell us anything specific or meaningful. While it is true that the architecture of many of the leading practices is itself fairly bland and undifferentiated, the language being used to describe it is even more so. Perhaps, you might argue, this is simply the marketing material, while the critical discussions about architecture are taking place elsewhere, for example in practices' design reviews or evening lectures. Unfortunately, there is little evidence that this is the case – very few architects are prepared to give properly researched lectures, preferring slide shows through a sequence of projects, while internal design reviews that sharpen the critical faculties are increasingly squeezed out of the routine of practice.

Apart from the negative impact on design and the ability of architects to explain their work, there are other dangers. Alex Gordon, a semiotician and CEO of Sign Salad, a branding agency specialising in cultural insight, believes that professionals are adopting the language of 'constructive ambiguity' as a way of avoiding being held to account:

> Architects, politicians, admen – everyone is 'delivering projects'; and everyone from plumbers to accountants and politicians offers 'bespoke solutions'. This language is being used to avoid locking businesses into a particular action.[18]

He warns that this gives a legal latitude that allows professionals to escape from commitment, and is fed from the desire to overcome the constriction of regulation: 'The language being used is so slippery, so ambiguous, that they are no longer committed to behaving in a particular way'.[19]

In other words, it is not that architects have adopted this language purely as a marketing tactic: the words they use reflect a shift in practice. Whether driven by commercial expediency, cultural pluralism or both, the danger is that architects are becoming more provisional and less committed in the way they operate as professionals.

Ironically, the emptiness of architectural dialogue – which is reflected in the way that architecture is discussed in magazines and within professional organisations – is welcomed as a means of making the profession more relevant and accessible. But the shortage of thoughtful writing by our leading architects is a real loss. It leaves practices open to the same criticism being levelled at corporations, local authorities and government – that their top-down, 'on-message' approach to communication underlies a lack of clarity and transparency about what they do.

Architectural writing by architects goes hand in hand with thinking and design. Language is an important way to develop knowledge and thinking about the discipline, and to enable others to understand its specific contribution. If architects themselves do not discuss architecture, who else will take responsibility for developing our understanding of the discipline? Introducing his book *Aesthetics & Architecture* (2007), Edward Winters points out that inhabiting architecture provides us with a sense of self and frames our 'lived world'. He continues with a useful warning: 'So we see that architecture is an art that involves us to a far greater extent than do the other arts. It is an art that we can ignore at the cost of diminishing our understanding of ourselves.'[20] ⋀

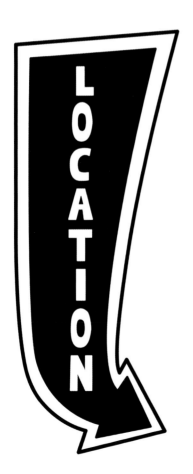

**Notes**
1. Adrian Forty, *Words and Buildings: A Vocabulary of Modern Architecture*, Thames & Hudson (London), 2000, p 13.
2. *Ibid*, p 22.
3. 'AJ100 2018 Survey': https://aj100awards.architectsjournal.co.uk/2018-ranking.
4. Forty, *op cit*, p 14.
5. Denise Scott Brown, 'Words About Architecture', *Having Words*, AA Publications (London), 2009, p 145.
6. www.scottbrownrigg.com/company/about/.
7. www.fosterandpartners.com/studio/our-approach/.
8. www.bdp.com/en/about/about-bdp/.
9. www.hawkinsbrown.com/about-us/approach.
10. www.sheppardrobson.com/practice.
11. Jeff Bradford, 'Bolstering Your Brand Through Vision and Mission Statements', *Forbes*, 24 August 2018: www.forbes.com/sites/forbesagencycouncil/2018/08/24/bolstering-your-brand-through-vision-and-mission-statements/#6c4da6ab2176.
12. https://grimshaw.global/practice/.
13. www.alliesandmorrison.com/practice/.
14. www.atkinsglobal.com/en-gb/corporate-sustainability/a-society-for-our-future.
15. Forty, *op cit*, p 114.
16. *Ibid*, p 115.
17. Alejandro Aravena, 'It's Time to Rethink the Entire Role and Language of Architecture', *The Guardian*, 20 November 2015: www.theguardian.com/cities/2015/nov/20/rethink-role-language-architecture-alejandro-aravena.
18. Interview with the author, 28 January 2019.
19. *Ibid*.
20. Edward Winters, *Aesthetics & Architecture*, Continuum (London), 2007, pp 10–11.

# A HYBRID PRACTICE MODEL

## EXPERT DIFFERENTIATION

The current and fast-moving intersection between architecture and technology has produced a welcome ambiguity in the role of the architect. So argues **Jenny E Sabin**, a Cornell University Professor and principal of the Jenny Sabin Studio in New York that explores these new market opportunities and finds them liberating for architects.

Jenny Sabin Studio,
*Lumen,*
MoMA PS1,
New York,
2017

Winner of the Museum of Modern Art's PS1 Young Architects Program,
*Lumen* is a socially and environmentally responsive structure that was held
in tension within the PS1 courtyard matrix of walls, applying insights and
theories from biology, materials science, mathematics and engineering.

It is well known that we are in the midst of a paradigm shift in architecture, one that is radically altering the tools that we employ to communicate information about form and space in the design process.[1] Plan, section, elevation – our primary visual notations for representing architecture for the past half-millennium – have been augmented by 3D animation, scripts, algorithms and building information models. These latter procedures inextricably connect precise geometry, contextual input, material constraints, fabrication logics and construction within architecture for the first time.

From the smooth spline in the 1990s, to the onset of digital fabrication and digital craft in the early 2000s, to the messiness of complexity and emergent design, and finally to the precision of data-driven information models, the instruments that we generate touch all aspects of architecture from generative diagram to fabricated component.[2] The signature styles that some of these digital strategies evoke simultaneously craft identity as they dominate and dictate the formal styles that we produce and promote online, in print and on social media.

Sabin Lab,
PolyBrick 2.0,
College of Architecture, Art, and Planning,
Cornell University,
Ithaca,
New York,
2017–19

Generated with the rules, principles and behaviour of bone formation, PolyBrick 2.0 makes use of algorithmic design techniques for the digital fabrication and production of nonstandard ceramic brick components for the mortarless assembly and installation of the first fully 3D-printed and fired ceramic brick assemblies.

Sabin+Jones LabStudio
(Jenny E Sabin, Andrew Lucia and
Peter Lloyd Jones),
*Branching Morphogenesis*,
SIGGRAPH,
Design and Computation Gallery,
Los Angeles,
2008

The installation materialised five slices in time
that captured the force network exerted by
interacting vascular cells upon their surrounding
matrix scaffold. Time is manifested as five vertical,
interconnected layers made from over 75,000 cable
zip-ties. The image won the AAAS/NSF International
Visualization Challenge and was featured on the
cover of *Science* in 2010.

As Mario Carpo points out, architects 'know that digital tools promise to eliminate all ambiguity from the laborious and always aleatoric process of architectural notation: a digital design file is ideally made for a mechanical recipient that does not interpret nor interpolate, but can only fabricate that which was scripted.'[3] The robot receives the code and the toolpath is executed. The powerful promise of a seamless transition from idea to materialised result opens a critical and reflexive ground that simultaneously influences the shape and form of our outward identities.

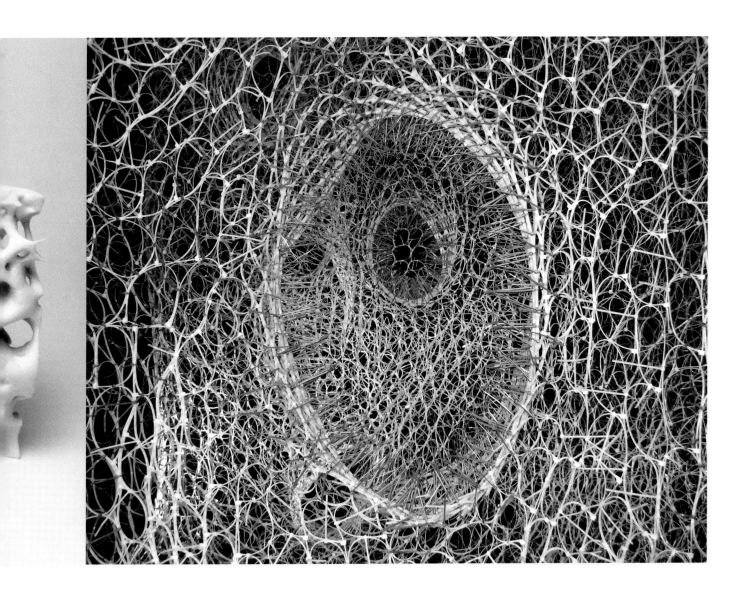

# The powerful promise of a seamless transition from idea to materialised result opens a critical and reflexive ground

While digital models and fabrication techniques are altering our formal landscape, design tooling is revolutionising how we think through a creative process. Scripted tools enable the architect to think systemically through the coordination of relationships – be they geometric, material, programmatic or otherwise.[4] In this context, and at the start of the 21st century, terms such as 'complexity', 'emergence' and 'dynamical' were being borrowed from science and associated with digital outputs that were subsequently defining architectural styles and shaping the culture of shared formal identities. Might we therefore learn from our colleagues in biology, materials science and beyond?

The Sabin+Jones LabStudio, jointly housed at the University of Pennsylvania's Institute for Medicine and Engineering and School of Design, and a collaboration with Peter Lloyd Jones (then an Associate Professor of Pathology and Laboratory Medicine at UPenn), was set up in 2006 to generate a collaborative space for design research between architecture and biology. The research undertaken quickly revealed that in addition to the many approaches that use science and nature for design inspiration, very little work had been formally established to examine reciprocal intersections between the individual fields.[5] An immediate bridge was through visualisation and communication. In fact, the very tools that were shaping identity in architecture became an important vehicle for generating expert differentiation and ultimately the generation of a hybrid practice model.

The Sabin Lab at Cornell University's College of Architecture, Art, and Planning in Ithaca, New York, has built upon this foundation, including the addition of an advanced degree in Matter Design Computation where students and faculty collaborate on shared research problems. In one project with Luo Labs at the university's Department of Biological and Environmental Engineering, for example,

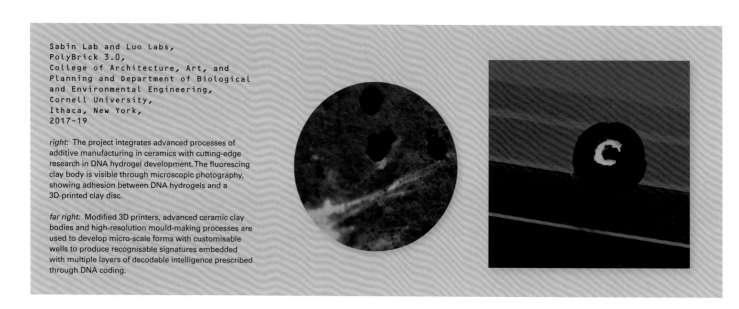

Sabin Lab and Luo Labs,
PolyBrick 3.0,
College of Architecture, Art, and
Planning and Department of Biological
and Environmental Engineering,
Cornell University,
Ithaca, New York,
2017–19

*right:* The project integrates advanced processes of additive manufacturing in ceramics with cutting-edge research in DNA hydrogel development. The fluorescing clay body is visible through microscopic photography, showing adhesion between DNA hydrogels and a 3D-printed clay disc.

*far right:* Modified 3D printers, advanced ceramic clay bodies and high-resolution mould-making processes are used to develop micro-scale forms with customisable wells to produce recognisable signatures embedded with multiple layers of decodable intelligence prescribed through DNA coding.

# Hybrid design thinking requires critical communication across disciplinary boundaries through shared processes, new ways of seeing, and within a pedagogical and discursive model

3D-printed ceramic blocks are differentiated via the first architectural component glazed with DNA hydrogel and impregnated with a living signature. Successful research results emanating from the lab are frequently applied in built projects, such as Jenny Sabin Studio's *Lumen* (2017) for MoMA PS1 in New York.

Computation, data-driven models and generative strategies are assets for approaching scientific problems as well as for creating a new culture of communication across disparate fields. Hybrid design thinking requires critical communication across disciplinary boundaries through shared processes, new ways of seeing, and within a pedagogical and discursive model in which architects and scientists collaborate in a shared lab and studio. In this context, ambiguity is a tool for new openings and identities in architecture and science. 𝝙

MEDstudio@JEFF and Jenny Sabin Studio,
THE BEACON: Focus on THE RAIL PARK,
Thomas Jefferson University,
Philadelphia,
Pennsylvania,
2016

A 6-metre (20-foot) tall, free-standing structure featuring responsive materials woven by drones in response to human interaction, the Beacon builds upon ongoing work at the intersection of architecture, health and medicine.

**Notes**
1. Mario Carpo, *The Alphabet and the Algorithm*, MIT Press (Cambridge, MA), 2011, pp 28–48, 81–106.
2. Scott Marble, 'Everything That Can Be Measured Will Be Measured', *TAD*, 2 (2), 2018, p 127.
3. Mario Carpo, 'The Art of Drawing', in Neil Spiller (ed), 𝝙 *Drawing Architecture*, September/October (no 5), 2013, pp 128–33.
4. Jenny Sabin and Peter Lloyd Jones, *LabStudio: Design Research Between Architecture and Biology*, Taylor & Francis/Routledge (London and New York), 2017, pp 35–8.
5. *Ibid*.

# THE MAN IN THE CONCRETE MASK

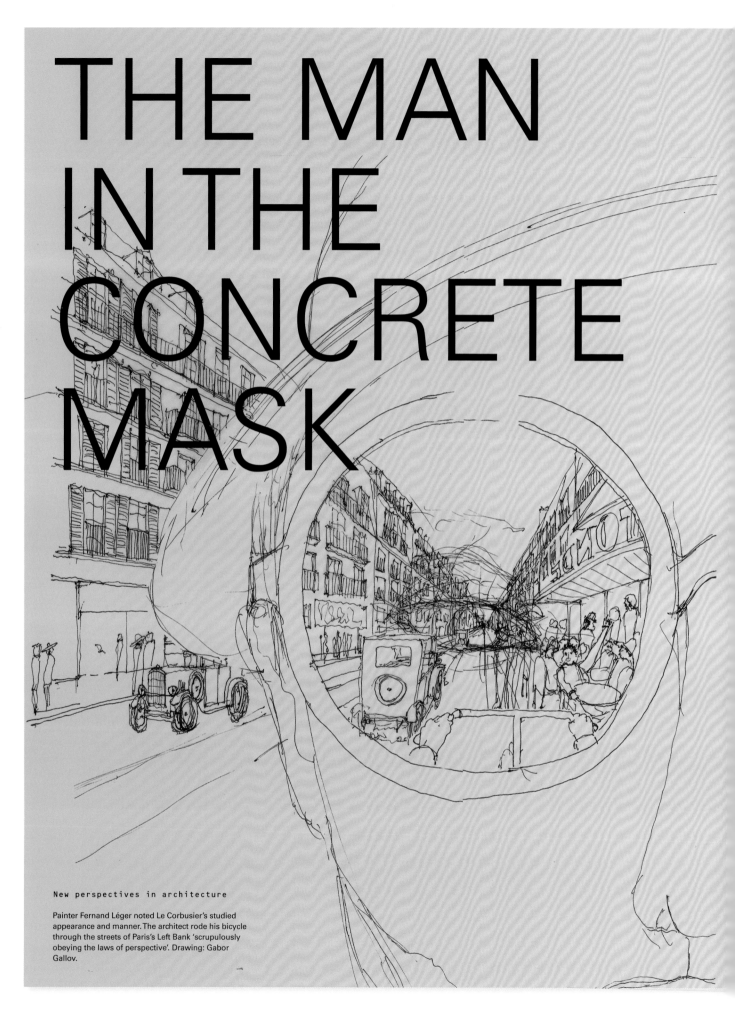

New perspectives in architecture

Painter Fernand Léger noted Le Corbusier's studied appearance and manner. The architect rode his bicycle through the streets of Paris's Left Bank 'scrupulously obeying the laws of perspective'. Drawing: Gabor Gallov.

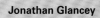
Jonathan Glancey

# The Metamorphosis of Charles-Édouard Jeanneret

How did Le Corbusier make the transition from mountain boy to modernist master? How did he develop his architectural persona and his design identity, and how did he communicate it to maximum effect? British journalist, author and broadcaster **Jonathan Glancey** leads us through some of the critical moments in Le Corbusier's rise to architectural immortality.

On 1 September 1907, Charles-Édouard Jeanneret came down from the mountains. He was 19 years old. This was his first trip away from the Calvinistic, French-speaking Swiss watch-making town of La Chaux-de-Fonds where he was born and brought up. His father engraved and enamelled watches and cases, his mother taught the piano. A skilled craftsman from the age of 15, and a budding artist, Jeanneret had already designed his first house, the Arts & Crafts Villa Fallet. It had been a student project.

Dropping down by train to Italy through the St Gotthard Pass, a copy of John Ruskin's *Mornings in Florence* (1875) to hand,[1] Jeanneret came to Florence via Lugano and Milan. Ruskin directed him outside the Renaissance city to the 14th-century Carthusian Charterhouse at Galluzzo. It was a moment of revelation. To Jeanneret, this beautiful yet restrained hillside complex comprising chaste individual houses and their gardens enclosed by a wall and giving on to a cloister, church, refectory and library seemed an ideal form of city housing as much as a remote and silent monastery. Offering both privacy and community and though comprising many individual elements, it was all of a piece.

Forty years later, the young Swiss craftsman's interpretation of this quietly haunting Florentine monastery would re-emerge on the fringe of Marseilles in the guise of l'Unité d'Habitation. This justly celebrated building was designed by the world-famous French architect Le Corbusier who, of course, had once been the quizzical and highly self-conscious Charles-Édouard Jeanneret.

Le Corbusier reading at home, Paris, May 1946

Portrait of the architect as artist: Le Corbusier photographed in his studio at home in 1946 by Nina Leen for *Life* magazine. Only rarely do we get to look behind the thick-lensed spectacles into the architect's eyes. Enigmatic as always, Le Corbusier stares straight back at us, revealing nothing of his inner complexity.

Railroad to discovery

In 1907, Charles-Édouard Jeanneret made his first trip away from home, by train from La Chaux-de-Fonds to Florence. The journey proved to be a revelation to the young craftsman-architect. Drawing: Gabor Gallov.

Le Corbusier,
Unité d'Habitation,
Marseilles,
France,
1952

*above:* The distinctive facade and skyline of the Unité d'Habitation apartment block reflect and animate a rational yet complex plan and interlocking section. The building is at once monastery, monument and social housing, an inspired melding of complex ideas nurtured by the architect over 40 years.

*below:* A secular 20th-century Parthenon for everyman. Roof structure and views from the top of the distinctive Marseilles apartment block reconcile modern architecture with the timeless and elemental surroundings of sea, sky and mountains.

The transformation of the young Swiss craftsman into the great French architect who was given a state funeral, and whose buildings and persona continue to haunt the architectural profession more than half a century after his death in 1965, is far more than merely interesting. Charles-Édouard Jeanneret's special genius was to invent and create the architect he wanted to be, and within a remarkably short time (between 1917, when he settled in Paris, and 1925) to make an international name as Le Corbusier, an architect with radical new ideas for houses, monumental architecture and cities. Le Corbusier was more than a mask, although by objectifying himself – as was fashionable among artists – Jeanneret was able to conceal his insecurities and depressions and to act the role of cultural provocateur, revolutionary designer and, as the years went by, sage, eminence and recluse.

Le Corbusier was also a badge, a shield, a marque that not only nurtured the architect's legend, but protected him to an extent from a life not always so very well lived. Somehow Le Corbusier, the abstract legend and creator of some of the most revered modern buildings of the 20th century – from the Villa Savoye at Poissy (1928–31) to the pilgrimage chapel at Ronchamp (1954–5) – was very much bigger than Charles-Édouard Jeanneret and his anti-Semitism, his professional association with the Pétain government, his easy company with Nazis, his keenness to work for Mussolini and his deep sense of worthlessness even when at the height of his creative powers.

## The Architect as *Objet-Type*

However brilliant a creation, Le Corbusier was definitely not a 'brand'. A brand, whether applied to a manufacturer of breakfast cereal or a modish architectural practice with an eye towards lucrative property development deals, uncritical media coverage and awards ceremonies, is a device suggesting that any or all products or buildings by such and such a manufacturer or practice are valuable and of a type, character and quality because the brand itself implies they are. 'Le Corbusier', on the other hand, suggested controversy, the gnomic and the unexpected. Most architects of any generation tend to toe the line whether technically, artistically, professionally, politically or socially. Le Corbusier did none of these things and yet was able to make his a powerful voice in modern architecture and to win commissions that were to range from private houses to large-scale residential schemes, parliamentary complexes, plans for new towns and cities, churches and, late in his career, a monastery.

For all the enigmatic and strangely compelling charisma of Le Corbusier – the architect as *objet-type* – Charles-Édouard Jeanneret observed keenly and drew distinctively and well. Fresh from his first travels in Italy, he knocked on the doors of the studios of architects in Paris. He met with almost immediate success. Auguste Perret, the pioneer of rational concrete design and construction, leafed through Jeanneret's Italian sketchbook and said: 'You will be my right hand.'[2]

There had been no need for a diploma or other professional qualifications. Perret could see that Jeanneret *saw*. The young man looked at buildings with his own eye, interpreted them and drew them in his own particular way. These drawings took him on to Berlin in 1910 and the studio of Peter Behrens where he worked with Walter Gropius and Mies van der Rohe. Restlessness and curiosity spurred Jeanneret to travel through the Balkans, to Istanbul and Athens where he discovered the Parthenon for himself and as if entirely anew.

For all the enigmatic and strangely compelling charisma of Le Corbusier – the architect as *objet-type* – Charles-Édouard Jeanneret observed keenly and drew distinctively and well

Le Corbusier,
*Nature morte au siphon* and
*Nature morte au hachoir*,
1928

Through painting, which he took up in earnest in 1918, Le Corbusier brought objects to life, making them, in his eyes, develop and metamorphose much as his architecture did. A constant play between painting, drawing and people created a distinct and constantly evolving aesthetic.

### Succès d'estime: the Paris Effect

Paris overwhelmed him at first. Largely penniless and something of an oddball he fell in, quite naturally, with the city's young artists. Amédée Ozenfant, a year older than Jeanneret and extensively travelled, encouraged his new friend to paint, which he did inventively and well. Cockily, the two young artists announced the birth of a new school – Purism – and by October 1920 had launched a lively and beautifully produced magazine, *L'Esprit Nouveau*. One of its authors was 'Le Corbusier', a play on the architect's grandmother's family name Lecorbésier and, perhaps, *corbeau* or crow, a bird known for its great intelligence and remarkable communication skills.

Le Corbusier drew and exhibited a model of a revolutionary white Purist house. This was Maison Citrohan (1920), a house that might be mass-produced like a Citroën car and not just for artists and the aesthetically inclined, but for people of all classes. It was something of a sensation. In line with his family motto *'Ce que tu fais, fais-le'* (never procrastinate),

Le Corbusier set up an architectural practice with his cousin Pierre Jeanneret. Serendipitously, or not, they moved in to a corridor of a Jesuit convent on rue de Sèvres.

With the help of Ozenfant, Le Corbusier published a manifesto, *Vers une Architecture* (1923), in which ocean liners, cars and aircraft shared pages, expositions and sentiments with Gothic cathedrals, the Parthenon and imminent new architecture. He designed and built the Maison La Roche-Jeanneret (1923–5), a two-part showcase for his work. One part was a Parisian house for his brother Albert, a musician, the other a studio and gallery for Raoul La Roche, a Swiss banker and collector of Cubist and Purist art Jeanneret had got to know during the First World War at the Déjeuner Suisse, a meeting place for Swiss exiles and émigrés. La Roche's studio-gallery, designed as a *Gesamtkunstwerk*, was a glamorous showcase for Le Corbusier's talents. Further Parisian houses followed as quickly as the architect's reputation grew. Even before the house was complete, Le Corbusier was busy organising publication of a 'Collected Works'.

By this time he had the met the painter Fernand Léger, a lifelong friend. Sat outside the fashionable café 'La Rotonde' – Picasso's studio was nearby – on the corner of Boulevard Montparnasse and Boulevard Raspail, Léger wryly observed Le Corbusier pedalling slowly towards him garbed in his newly defining bowler hat, bow tie and thick-framed owlish round glasses from Maison Bonnet. 'This object,' noted Léger, 'advanced on its bicycle scrupulously obeying the laws of perspective.'[3]

As La Roche held cocktail parties for the fashionable wealthy at his new studio-gallery home, Le Corbusier designed the Esprit Nouveau pavilion for the 1925 Exposition Internationale des Arts Décoratifs et Industriels Modernes, a World's Fair, held on both banks of the Seine. Considered scandalous even by exhibition organisers, the pavilion was something of a *coup de théâtre* for the architect. Inside and out it demonstrated Le Corbusier's ideas for exacting mass housing. Inside, too, was a diorama of his Plan Voisin, or Paris reimagined as a partly high-rise city. Hugely controversial, perhaps even today, this was a rousing provocation that made the name Le Corbusier both famous and infamous. Over the course of six months, 16 million people from around the world visited the 1925 exhibition.

Gabriel Voisin, the inventive aircraft and automobile engineer, financed Le Corbusier's iconoclastic city plan. The architect took to driving distinctive Voisin cars and having them photographed with his latest buildings. This was not simply to curry favour with his patron, but also to demonstrate the relationship between cars and architecture – 'a house is a machine for living in' – and to show an affinity with the latest and most adventurous engineering design.

During this extraordinary period in which he became famous, Le Corbusier developed a way of giving talks, using charcoal, chalk and pencils to draw as he spoke, so that lectures were not a reflection on design and architecture, but an active and creative part of their process. It was an ingenious way of revealing a genius for design.

Purist party,
Maison La Roche-Jeanneret,
Paris

Designed with his cousin Pierre Jeanneret, this two-part Parisian villa (1923–5) for Raoul La Roche, a Swiss banker and collector of Cubist and Purist art, was a showcase for Le Corbusier's radical architecture. At cocktail parties here, Le Corbusier was introduced to the artistic beau-monde and members of a self-conscious avant-garde, some becoming clients for his experimental white villas. Drawing: Gabor Gallov

### L'Étranger: a Stranger in the World

All this said, it seems important to remember that Le Corbusier the public man was also Charles-Édouard Jeanneret, in his own words 'a stranger in the world', neither particularly keen on a social life nor much interested in money, property, possessions or social climbing. 'We do not work to be praised,' he said shortly before he died swimming into the sun at Roquebrune-Cap-Martin, 'we work out of duty to our conscience'.[4] Significantly, he liked to believe that he was descended from purist Cathars who had escaped to Switzerland from Papal persecution in the 13th century. More ambitiously, he wanted to change the world through architecture.

Of his image and the way he was seen by the media, Le Corbusier had indeed worked hard, imaginatively and very quickly to establish an identity as compelling as it was truly his own. No agency, no marketing company, no consultant could have invented Le Corbusier. He was a creation of his own making. Clearly he understood the importance of making a mark beyond the immediacy of the buildings he designed and plans he promulgated. There have been and continue to be very good and even exceptional architects who either have no particular interest in publicity or no ability to promote themselves to a wider world.

Equally, Le Corbusier, although exceptional, was not alone. Frank Lloyd Wright was a master of his own myth-making, as was, in a calm, cool and economical way, Mies van der Rohe. Treasured by Le Corbusier, Ruskin's writings on architecture were much influenced by Augustus Welby Pugin, a firecracker of a man, architect and designer who wrote glorious, slashing polemics that gained him attention and encouraged commissions. From the late 1830s, Pugin created an enchanting world of revived medieval art and Catholic society on paper that he got to build. Visitors to his Ramsgate studio expected to find a priest-like man working in monkish quietude. The architect they actually met was lively, funny and nothing like a cleric, which was not surprising given that Pugin had learned as much of his scenic skills working in the Covent Garden theatre as he had from drawing medieval buildings from life.

In his own English Victorian way, Pugin knew exactly how to create the public persona capable of winning the commissions he dreamed of. Again, though, like Le Corbusier his was an image that could not have been invented by anyone else, and it would have failed to work had he not been such a persuasive draughtsman and pugnacious polemicist. While architecturally Le Corbusier was by far the greater talent, like Pugin he was not an intellectual. He, too, was a man of faith and emotion whose ideal commissions were churches and monasteries or mass housing informed by the design of medieval charterhouses.

It is quite possible that Le Corbusier chose the timing and setting of his death. The young man who came down from the Swiss mountains in 1907 wanted to be in control of his persona, his image and his destiny. To a remarkable degree he succeeded. His success, though, was due mostly to his innate talent, his sense of adventure and his ability to look and to draw and to focus on what truly mattered to him. Nobody could have made Le Corbusier except Charles-Édouard Jeanneret. △

**Notes**
1. John Ruskin, *Mornings in Florence: Simple Studies of Christian Art for English Travellers*, George Allen (Orpington), 1875.
2. Maximilien Gauthier, *Le Corbusier, ou l'architecture au service de l'homme*, Éditions Denoël (Paris), 1944, p 28.
3. Jean Petit, *Le Corbusier lui-même*, Éditions Rousseau (Geneva), 1970, p 54.
4. Recording of Le Corbusier made by Hugues Desalle, 25 May 1965. Vinyl LP, Réalisations Sonores Hugues Desalle, France, 1965.

# Worldcraft

## Building Worlds
## One Project
## at a Time

BIG (Bjarke Ingels Group),
Greenland National Gallery of Art, Nuuk,
Greenland,
2011

Just like in fiction, BIG invites people into a strange yet familiar
world when presenting renderings, animations and spoken or
written words to the public. They flesh out a world that feels
real and relatable through its setting, plot, language, characters
and mood, and embed an element of fantasy for each project.

Over the last decade, Copenhagen- and New York-based architecture and urbanism firm Bjarke Ingels Group (BIG) has enjoyed a meteoric rise on the world stage. **Daria Pahhota** has presided over this as its Chief Communications Officer, heading the team that decides where, when and how the practice disseminates its news, messages and personality. Here she gives us a glimpse behind the scenes.

Bjarke Ingels at the
'Future of Storytelling',
New York,
2014

BIG founder Bjarke Ingels lying on a drawing created by him for a documentary describing his 'worldcraft' concept, which is similar to the 'worldbuilding' used in film and fiction to create imaginary worlds.

BIG (Bjarke Ingels Group),
KLM – The Clover Block,
Copenhagen,
2006

This proposal to solve a housing shortage without losing any of the city's beloved green space through a 'Chinese wall' of residences put Bjarke Ingels and BIG on the map.

The question I get asked most often as BIG's Chief Communications Officer is: 'What is your communication strategy?' The honest answer is that we do not have a strategy. Instead, we operate on a number of principles and values for all our internal and external communications across a variety of channels.

When I joined BIG in 2008, as a young communications student from Copenhagen Business School, the company was already on a fast track: Bjarke Ingels, who founded the practice in 2005, had several significant commissions under his belt, and most locals in Copenhagen had either heard about the studio because of its ingenious proposal to solve a housing shortage without losing any of the city's beloved green space through a 'Chinese wall' of residences, or through Bjarke's involvement in a loaded public debate about high-rises.

Already by then, the 50-person Copenhagen-based studio had a strong visual and verbal language that felt raw, completely fearless and transparent. BIG was unafraid to expose the often-messy design process, making politicians, users and neighbours – happy or angry – part of the process. Until that point, I personally only knew architecture as renderings or finished buildings. In a true eureka moment, BIG unlocked a new world for me, where buildings had personalities and lives of their own.

Bjarke Ingels,
TED Talk,
Vancouver,
2009

BIG's profile and exposure have increased at high speed since the studio's foundation in 2005.

Over the next few years, BIG and our communication efforts evolved at a start-up pace, accelerating in 2010 following the opening of the Shanghai Expo Pavilion and the 8 House completion in Ørestad. Lots of new faces, ideas and projects came and went, as did most efforts at controlling the explosive development. Any written-down strategy got old before it was adopted. Despite the rapid change, the strong foundation and principles we had set early on remained. For example, at BIG we want to show, not tell, and we don't 'show' until we have all the critical visual assets such as renderings and diagrams to share the stories born through projects. We want to contribute to a positive discourse, to be understood by an audience who does not speak the language of floor plans or axonometrics. We are all authors in the work. These principles combined create a generous yet clear framework for BIG to control the messaging of each project despite their differences. They also set a really high bar for when and how BIG talks about the studio's work to the public.

How does this translate to communication at an operational level? Over the years, BIG has created an ever-developing multi-channel platform including books, conferences, press releases, animations, websites and branding for articulating and sharing news about the studio in a way that lets people into the chaos while providing them with essential information to understand the project, hopefully like it and help spread the word. Specifically, we dive deep and tailor a communications strategy for each individual project – a micro-strategy.

The success of these campaigns goes back to BIG's design process. Following extensive research, project teams identify a single intrinsic question that is then answered through design. For example, the BIG U flood-protection system in downtown Manhattan asks: 'Can protective measures become the city's attractions which both protect and serve as upgrades for the social and urban fabric?' It is the clarity and the sharpness of both question and answer – our design – that fuels the communications team's ability to share the unique identity and narrative for each project with the public. BIG's magic is not limited to telling a good story; it lies also in the studio's ability to construct a desirable world for each project, leaving no gaps for our audience to 'fill' in, and making them homesick for a place they have never been. Δ

BIG (Bjarke
Ingels Group),
The BIG U,
New York City,
2014

The BIG U flood-protection system's design answers the question of whether protective measures can become the city's attractions, both protecting and upgrading its social and urban fabric. It gives the BIG communications team some very clear pointers as to what to focus on.

# OBSERVATIONS ON DRAWING

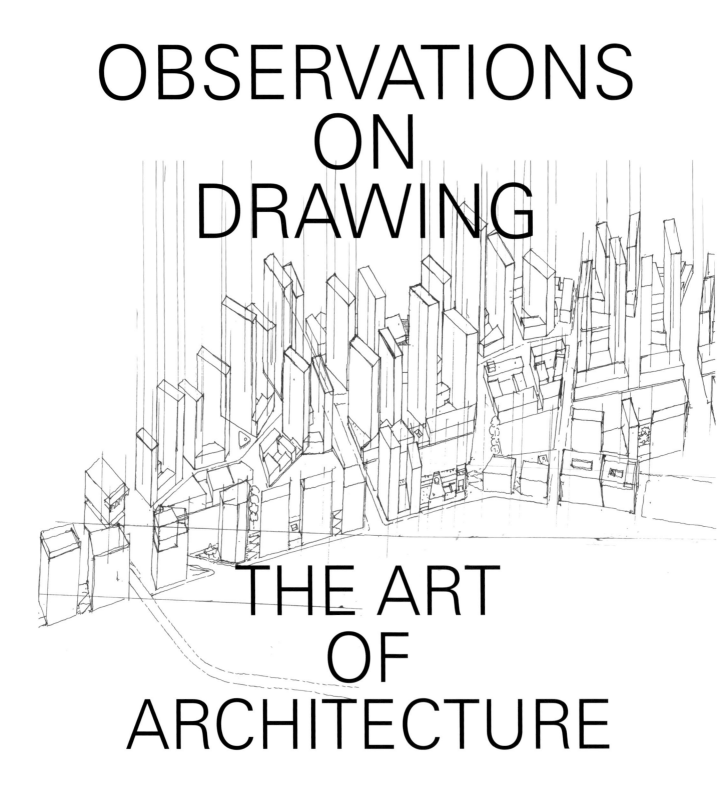

# THE ART OF ARCHITECTURE

A hand-drawn urban-scale diagram investigating
the spatiality of a proposal.

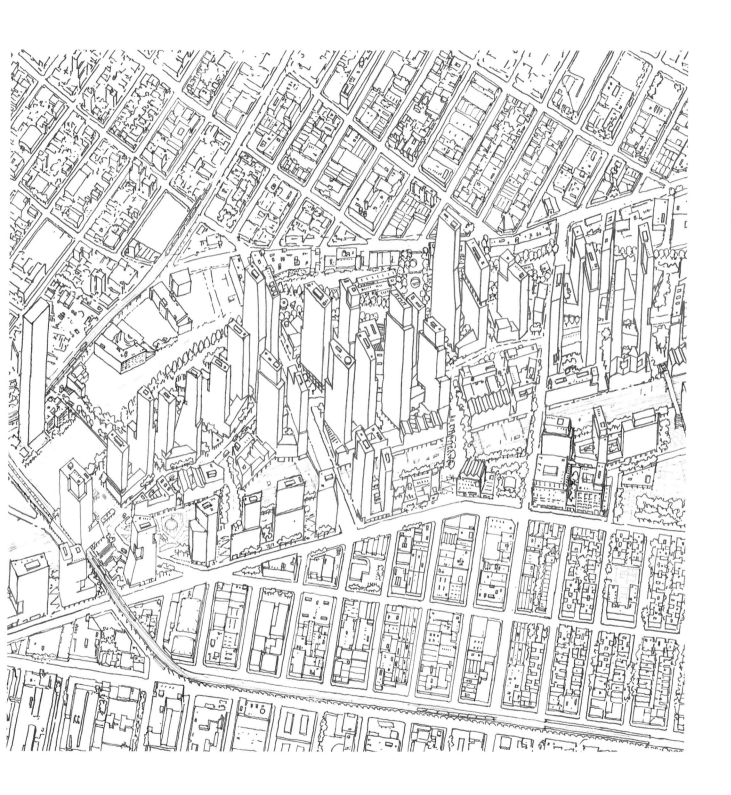

How important is the sketch and the hand drawing to the identity of the architect two decades into the 21st century? London-based architect and architectural tutor **Gabor Gallov** argues it is still as crucial as it always was in conveying ideas, but equally as a vehicle for exploring the subtleties of individual architectural language away from the ubiquitous computer and rendering.

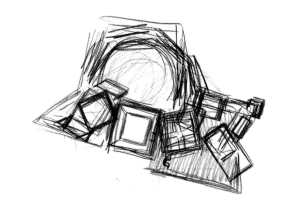

Louis Kahn,
Dominican Motherhouse,
Media, Pennsylvania,
1967

The sketch reveals the layering of thought process and areas of focus, and depicts the overall thesis of the project whilst simultaneously in development. A representation of the author's identity.

This student is nervous presenting his work. It is 10.45 am. He has not slept or eaten. He is babbling through his presentation, pointing to computer-generated SketchUp® images that have little to do with what he is muttering to the review panel. His ideas have not survived the process along which he travelled to formulate his architectural conclusions in the third dimension. The hapless student absorbs the confused stares of the review panel which, in turn, makes him further unsure and even less coherent. He finally concludes the presentation and stands back exhaling.

We start asking questions and picking through his scattered portfolio that is supposed to record the process of his thinking and the development of the project. As expected he receives a scathing review. His stare reflects worry mixed with defeat mitigated only by the fact that his 'all-nighter' is at least finally over. Almost. It is my turn to ask questions and whilst I prefer to tutor students by positive encouragement, I point to a small sketch in his little portfolio and yell, 'What is this?!!' The room falls silent for in today's politically correct English universities, yelling at a student is equal to assaulting a minor. I shout once again 'What in Hell is this??' pointing at a small pencil-and-crayon doodle. He mutters, looking at it embarrassedly, 'It's only a sketch, to express and record my preliminary ideas.'

The student is ready to faint from nervousness and fatigue when I shout one final time: 'This is unbelievably beautiful! It's amazing! You did this? You could remove your whole presentation from the board and pin up this tiny hand sketch. It would explain everything without you even being present. It encapsulates your ideas, your process and, above all, it's a hundred times stronger than the pitiful attempt at realistic presentation with a computer program. If you can draw like this what on earth are you puttering about with a mouse?' The student begins to show a glimmer of hope, of light. Perhaps there is something good coming out of this after all. He has an excuse though: the usual, 'The school's encouraging me to do this.' I reply, crashing things back down to earth, 'That is a cop-out answer!'

One of my favourite experiences teaching architecture studio is when students who are temporarily weaned off the computer begin to realise that their hand drawings improve in a matter of weeks if not days. They discover that they can express ideas

Oscar Cheng,
Museum of Water: Phenomena, Atmosphere,
Detail, 3rd-year final project,
Nottingham Trent University,
2014

The student's manual drawing style, here in pencil, importantly reveals more of the ideas than being masked by computer-generated precision and finality. (This is not the student described in the article.)

clearly and yet in tantalising ways that resist finality or singularity, and that this is OK. But my very favourite moment is when they pin up at an interim review and realise that their drawings are quite different from their fellow students', that they possess a singularity representative of themselves. A signature, an identity. I love that smirk.

Today's cultural and commercial world demands the rapid communication of ideas through fancy images produced at speed. But speed steals identity. One discovers oneself through the act of manual drawing. Of course to some extent we need to get students ready for the professional world they are about to enter, but it has to be done in a measured way – because the proper development of a creative architectural mind and identity can rarely be acquired later, whilst understanding and utilising, say, Revit, V-Ray and building information modelling (BIM) can.

Joseph Gandy,
*A Bird's-Eye View of the Bank of England,*
1830

Gandy's ruinous illustration was exhibited by Sir John Soane himself at London's Royal Academy in 1830 to portray his more than four decades of work on the Bank of England, as its official architect and surveyor (1788–1833). The manner and style of depiction is at once a form of public relations, identification of identity and influencer of approach to further work.

Paul Rudolph,
Yale Art and
Architecture Building,
New Haven,
Connecticut,
1963

*above:* The hatched lines of this drawing determined the materiality of the cladding: ribbed concrete.

*right:* This drawing's hatched lines express absorbed light and the aspiration of verticality in the composition.

## Heroes

It used to be pleasurable looking at magazines and guessing which architectural firm proposed which building simply by observing their presentation style. Today, with a multitude of CGI software, it is quite difficult, as images from different practices can seem very similar, with authorship and identity washed away. The only chance of expressing identity then remains in creating buildings with exaggerated form, with their 'iconic' status heralded in the media. To some degree this is due to the fact that many talented design partners need to part with their 'child' quickly as the project is swiftly computer imaged and presented to the adoptive client as finality whilst being fed into BIM. One must ask, how could the talent, sometimes the creative madness of a unique architect survive this sequence of delivery and be present in the built result? We hear of Louis Kahn or Frank Lloyd Wright visiting sites and sometimes making the kinds of subtle finishing decisions that nudge great architecture into the realm of the sublime. These days, the delicate decisions of a talented author making late changes to even a medium-sized project are unheard of.

Architectural history is riddled with offices that nurtured a culture of high-quality draughtsmanship that became an essential part of their identity. Sir Christopher Wren, Sir John Soane, Charles Francis Annesley Voysey, Richard Rogers, Norman Foster, Zaha Hadid: all of these studios had a strong connection to drawing and painting which fed back into the development of their buildings and vice versa. Drawings became, in modern terms, an internal public-relations exercise beyond external PR, influencing and nurturing internal office cultures beyond 'house style'. Sir John Soane's buildings painted as Roman ruins by his artist draughtsman Joseph Gandy in the early 1800s were PR exercises in identity. They also fed back and further influenced later buildings. The 20th-century American modernist Paul Rudolph's linear hatched heavy perspective drawings were manifested in ribbed concrete details and an almost overwhelming sense of spatiality. Truly great architects' drawings manifested themselves as spatial signatures.

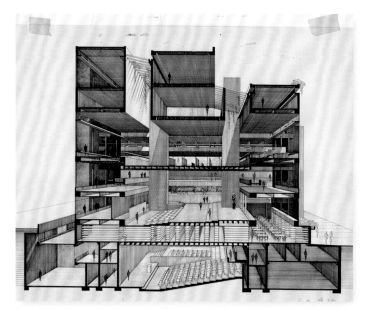

Paul Rudolph,
Yale Art and Architecture Building,
New Haven,
Connecticut,
1963

*above:* Section drawing showing a distinctive spatial interpretation aspired to by the architect.

*below:* Photograph showing the unique and distinctive signature spatial overlap and interpenetration inherent throughout the building.

# Quietness and subtlety are the opposites of the hunger of embryonic parametric software and CAD-only-reared design

## Practice

A particular office that held onto its identity throughout its growth is cited here for two reasons. One is that I had the privilege to be a part of this office and observe its growth first hand. The second reason will become apparent at the end of the next few paragraphs. If it has lost some of its identity over the years, it is only a result of being so widely copied.

When I entered the British firm of Allies and Morrison, the culture of the office was steeped in a careful, polite and thoughtful style of drawings. The muted drawing style could be observed in the early sketches of the partners and it was ultimately translated into the presentations destined for clients. The consideration of line weights and quietness of presentations, whether inked or eventually computer drawn, were painfully guarded. This attention was subsequently channelled into detail drawings for construction, affecting the choice of details and materials. There is no doubt that the procurement stage was then also influenced by this calm attention. One can say that many buildings of the practice to this day stand as forms of fine and considered drawings. This particular culture of drawings looped back to feed the generation of new projects and guide new employees entering the growing practice. It was, in a sense, an internal PR exercise as well as a way of designing and building.

It is true that the style and identity of a practice can also be a form of control. With the amount of projects entering a firm, the consistency of an internal house style can be a way to maintain signature, quality and focus even when designs inevitably begin to be delegated to secondary leaders and their teams.

The second reason for citing this office is that their identity does not manifest in exaggerated forms of building. It emerges as quietness and subtlety. This can only be a result of maintaining this particular culture of calm drawing as the guiding process. Subtlety cannot be born out of beginning and developing a building project only on computers. Quietness and subtlety are the opposites of the hunger of embryonic parametric software and CAD-only-reared design. The same applies here as in the world of haute cuisine; Enrique Olvera, owner and masterchef of the world-renowned Pujol restaurant in Mexico City, offered this advice to aspiring young chefs: 'Don't be in a hurry. When you hurry things in the kitchen, they end up not being so good. Take your time. Cook slowly. Enjoy the process.'[1]

I have left behind my short stint with Allies and Morrison but spoke recently to a senior design partner, Alfredo Caraballo. Alfredo is responsible for the firm's large to very large projects and he has a somewhat different yet related process of design to that of the founding partners. His particular approach to composition and spatiality is at an urban level through which he is guiding the firm towards new horizons. I asked him how the identity of the practice is maintained, if at all possible at an urban scale and if manual drawings still had a significant role to play. Alfredo says that maintaining the identity of a large practice and of large projects is quite difficult but that hand drawing is still an essential day-to-day practice within the company. He explains that there is a much better understanding and judgement of urban spatiality, context and structure when it is engaged through manual means as it is more connected to how the eye actually sees and how the body experiences and absorbs the urban realm.

Alfredo noted that there is no design process established in the office where the hand sketch is transformed into client-consumable images as quickly as possible. On many projects the drawings are

Jessica Booth,
Gesamtkunstwerk: A Boutique Hotel,
3rd-year final project,
Nottingham Trent University,
2015

The manual drawing style importantly reveals the atmosphere and ideas of its author rather than being masked and overtaken by the identity of global presentation software.

further elaborated in detail, remaining in hand-drawn format, and even when they are inevitably transformed into computer drawings they are reprinted and further worked on and affected by hand. He believes that the tools used affect the development of the project and that these processes do eventually become embodied in the detailing and decision-making, therefore forming a part of the identity of the project and ultimately of the practice. He likens this process to calligraphy. He has also revealed that clients, even on large projects, are more likely to ask if they can keep the hand sketches rather than the CGI images, as they contain a human connection to the work.

## Resisting the Urge to Use the Word 'Resisting'

We can now see presentation software with fantastic amounts of computational memory, more than that required to land a man on the Moon, pedalling very hard to make images look as if they may have been hand drawn and 'quietly painted'. A surreal amount of computation to make the end result imperfect and human; how odd is that? But they all look much the same. We have entered a phase of architecture where many founding partners cannot actually draw by hand and an almost global scale of identity is emerging, language defined by the limits and tricks of rendering and form-producing programs.

Maintaining a culture of hand drawing in schools and architecture schools, small practices and even large firms is good for architecture. Refusing to fully trade thoughtful, intimate human connection to the work for speed and quicker procurement of the project is a route to keeping one's identity and indeed the profession's identity. I have been resisting the urge to use the word 'resistance' in this essay. Retaining manual interaction through the development of architectural works is not a matter of resistance, nostalgia, or an act of neo-Luddism. Rather, it is perhaps best described as wanting to maintain the very *art* of architecture. ᴆ

**Note**
1. Quoted by Justin H Min in 'Modern Mexican: Enrique Olivera of Pujol' (interview), *Cereal*, 15, Spring/Summer 2018, p 32.

Allies and Morrison,
Sarum Hall School,
London,
1993

The drawing depicts the careful editing and layering of the design which has character yet subdued emotion.

# The Personal is Universal

## On Aldo Rossi's Autobiography

Italian architect Aldo Rossi's rise to fame, and recognition by professionals and public alike, was predicated on him putting across his personal passions and memories of life experience. Italian-born, London-based architect and tutor **Robin Monotti Graziadei** investigates how the intertwining of architecture with the personal imperatives of the architect produced some extraordinary work.

Aldo Rossi and Claude Züber,
Stage set design
for Donizetti's
*Lucia di Lammermoor,*
Ravenna,
1986

Aldo Rossi believed that it was events that animated architecture, and that therefore architecture followed the example set by theatre.

'To understand the city in a concrete way means to grasp the individuality of its inhabitants – an individuality that is the basis of the monuments themselves.'

— Aldo Rossi, *The Architecture of the City*, 1966[1]

Cover of *Domus* magazine,
no 602,
January 1980

The cover featured a portrait of Aldo Rossi by Occhiomagico, edited by Emilie van Hees.

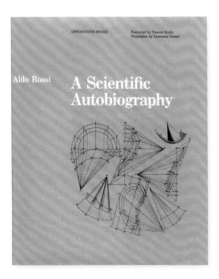

Aldo Rossi,
Cover of *A Scientific Autobiography*,
The MIT Press,
1981

Cover of Aldo Rossi's autobiography which was written in the form of notes over a 10-year period, featuring a drawing by Guarino Guarini: *Architettura Civile*, plate 38.

In *Notre-Dame de Paris* (1831) – better known in English as *The Hunchback of Notre-Dame* – Victor Hugo's Archdeacon claims that the book will destroy the edifice.[2] Sixty-five years later the Lumière brothers invented cinematography and since then film became the preferred candidate to destroy book and edifice. Architecture, though, remained alive by largely operating through the visual imagination rather than via direct engagement with the edifice. In this world of the architectural imagination, fictional architects in film are also arguably better at capturing the interest of the public than most real architects themselves. Why? Perhaps because films with architects in leading roles are written by non-architects and are rarely about architecture itself. More often, they are about events that happen around buildings and about architects as human beings rather than as simply cogs in a professional wheel.

There are of course exceptions. Aldo Rossi captivated an entire segment of both the profession and the wider public through drawings and writings even more than through his buildings. This asymmetrical success story is useful not in teaching architects how to make better buildings, but in how to appeal to a wider public when talking about them. Rossi wrote about his life and projects in *A Scientific Autobiography* (1981), a dreamlike book in which analogies with other works and personal passions take centre stage as paths to revealing the significance of architectural projects.[3] What art and architecture have in common, says Rossi, is that they are both born in unconscious life. By reaching into a deep well of personal memories, he describes his projects not simply as objects, but as labours of love rooted in his personal history.

As the 'Scientific' part of his title indicates, Rossi's is a book written to elucidate the thinking behind his projects rather than a conventional life story. His mind reveals itself as harbouring a world of analogies, where everything refers to something else yet everything ultimately is rooted in what the architect and writer holds most precious. Rossi encourages architects to write about what they love rather than describing projects in words in a formal and detached way, and that is how he is able to connect to a wider audience.

## Analogy

Lessons for architects that could be extracted from Rossi's use of analogy could be summarised in a set of suggestions: when writing about a project, find ways of describing it by referring to other things beyond it, preferably not other modern or contemporary projects that only architects know. Historical buildings or cities can be referenced freely as these tap into a body of shared experiences with non-architects. Allow these links to indicate further associations and these to multiply even further. When referring to autobiographical experiences make sure to address their civic or socially shared dimension so as to go beyond the purely personal and into the universal. Addressing the connection and relations between the project under discussion and links beyond it creates new meanings. The description itself becomes a creative project. This creative dimension in Rossi's writing is what keeps descriptions interesting and stops them fossilising into formulae that can easily fail to interest non-architects.

## Atmosphere

Rossi's notion of atmosphere is derived from the Italian word *tempo*, which means both time and weather. His approach is to reference specific times of day and specific weather when discussing his projects. He describes fog entering Leon Battista Alberti's Basilica of Sant'Andrea in Mantua (begun 1472), then links this to memories of seeing fog penetrate the Galleria Vittorio Emanuele II in Milan (1877) and how it changes the perception of the architecture and of the people within it. Referring to his San Cataldo Cemetery design in Modena (1971) he describes it, even before it took shape, as belonging to the atmosphere defined by the extensive mists of the Po valley and to houses on the riverbank abandoned after great floods. In this way, the idea of atmosphere as time and weather is the connecting element between site location and project, creating an uninterrupted link between observation and design which he then articulates in words to draw the reader into a specific atmosphere before, or even in place of, any other approach to the description of a project.

## Imagination

If architecture can be seen as a form of technique for the creation of buildings, then Rossi asks the question: What is the aim of this technique in relation to our understanding? What he implies is that we do not simply build in order to make buildings. We build in order to make buildings that we can then understand. How do we understand a building? We need to match it to something that already exists, or partially exists, in our imagination or in our memory. If we fail to do so we make a building that will neither be understood nor appreciated on all levels. For this reason, Rossi believed that the aim of all technique, architecture included, is the identification of the object, or the building, with our imagination. If the aim of the project beyond its physical and practical purposes is to capture the imagination, we then should be appealing directly to this imagination in its description. To do this we need to tap into a set of memories shared with non-architects. Memory becomes a key guiding element of the design process.

## Memory

Rossi's design process relies on projecting a memory onto the perception of a location, and watching the ensuing reaction between the two take place during the development of a project. The ability to describe the initial memory is essential for a successful project description. According to Rossi, reality is perceived via our individual memory's ability to recognise what belongs to the self and what is foreign to it. When what is recognised as the self can be shared with others, a relation between the self and the other is created which brings down barriers between the two. This is the area that Rossi aimed to cover in his project descriptions, and shared memories are one of the strongest common grounds we can have with others, therefore they are what writing ultimately aims to recreate in establishing the relation between writer and reader.

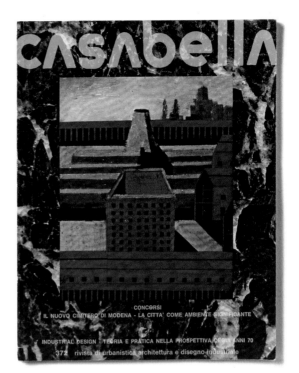

Cover of *Casabella* magazine,
no 372,
December 1972

This *Casabella* issue featured the competition for San Cataldo Cemetery in Modena (1971), and a drawing of Aldo Rossi's project for it featured on the cover.

Giuseppe Mengoni,
Galleria Vittorio Emanuele II,
Milan,
1877

Italy's oldest active shopping arcade was a reference for Aldo Rossi in the way it allows the weather to vary the atmosphere within.

Aldo Rossi,
*Composition with Gallaratese housing, Modena cemetery and Theatre of the World,*
1979

Following the precedent set by Canaletto's *Capriccio with Palladian Buildings* (1756–9), Aldo Rossi drew this and other compositions featuring his own projects in analogous cities of his own creation.

Aldo Rossi,
Molteni Funerary
Chapel,
Giussano,
1987

The theme of mortality was a recurring thread in Aldo Rossi's work and he completed this small chapel 16 years after his San Cataldo Cemetery project in Modena.

Rossi also invites us to describe ourselves and our work from the point of view of being human rather than representatives of a profession

## Mortality

We all share an awareness of mortality and this is an area that Rossi describes at length specifically with reference to his Modena cemetery project. For Rossi, the pursuit of architectural representation is in itself a way of addressing the issue of mortality. Building for the long term is one way of facing mortality positively and constructively. For Rossi cities are places for both the living and the dead, where fragments and elements of the dead act as signals and warnings to the living. The awareness of mortality relates to the entire cycle of life, and does not have to be negative when talked about with reference to a project. The circular way that Rossi uses to achieve this is by referring back to memories of the experiences of childhood. For Rossi it is to childhood that the phenomenological separation between the self and the world can be traced, and this is the separation experienced by the architect between the project as merely a representation and the project as a completed and lived building. The architect inhabits an extended childhood experience of separation between the self and the world throughout the design process. This is a fertile area for recollections of the different stages of life we all share, bringing in the specificities of our individual imagination and how these led us to become the architects we are now.

## Theatre

Rossi loved the theatre and saw in it a strong analogy with architecture. Theatre and film are fertile areas of shared memories. Given the large common ground between theatre, film and architecture, architects can look to these as areas of study. Rossi saw in theatre an art that could be lived to the full. He was interested by the power theatre has to illustrate and change a situation of relationships between human beings, which was also the ambition he harboured for his architecture. For Rossi, it is the event that takes place in a building that is architecture, not the inert object. There can be no theatre without an event, therefore there can also be no architecture without an event, which can of course also be the event of experiencing architecture itself.

## Writing

The latent argument in Rossi's autobiography is that writing is itself a project requiring a specific design approach. Writing should not be an afterthought. The design approach to writing in Rossi's view works best when it reveals aspects not evident in the architecture, so as to complement it rather than merely duplicate in words what is already on paper or indeed built. A project description should not be the chronological account of the design process if the goal is to interest anybody who is not a practising architect. The design approach that Rossi takes in writing about architecture is to talk about architecture as a writer, as a film or theatre director, or as a painter rather than as an architect. Paradoxically, Rossi believed that through this disassociation of techniques he would be able to get closer to an identification of the creative process with the project in question than if he were to write purely physical descriptions of projects.

The project description becomes a form of encounter between people, architecture and reality which in itself becomes a projection of the architect. What this means is that the description should go *beyond* architecture in order to enter into a form of *mimesis* or imitation of the experience of architecture, which is most often tangential. A direct perception of an entirety of an inert physical mass on the scale of a building is not only impossible for our senses, it is also the least interesting aspect to focus on as it is the most static and isolated approach.

Returning to cinema and taking the lead from Rossi's disassociation of techniques, architecture could be described through the approach that Michelangelo Antonioni took in representing the eclipse in his film *L'Eclisse*.[4] Shot during the year of the solar eclipse of 1961, there is the sense here of a narrative leading to an impending eclipse, literal and metaphorical. When it comes to the scene which represents the time of the eclipse, Antonioni films everything that is happening or, in this case, not happening between the characters. He films the streets of Rome. You see light levels subtly changing. You sense that an eclipse may be happening and its projected atmosphere and aura is touching everything else that is happening on screen, yet this is achieved without ever turning the camera towards the solar eclipse itself in the entire film.

Rossi invites us to write and talk about architecture as if we were Antonioni shooting a film about an eclipse, by doing this tangentially and indirectly and, in so doing, addressing the motivations of why architects choose to pursue the design of specific buildings in the first place, rather than shifting all the emphasis onto the object.

Rossi also invites us to describe ourselves and our work from the point of view of being human rather than representatives of a profession with all its unofficial codes of communication, and to describe our relationship to the world and others in a way that complements the architecture rather than duplicates it. Through his deeply personal autobiography, Rossi does not intend to indicate a single approach to writing about architecture: his example opens the doors to creative writing approaches that lead in many different directions, helping to break through unnecessary barriers between the architectural community and the wider audiences of non-professionals. ∞

**Notes**
1. Aldo Rossi wrote this with reference to Claude Lévi-Strauss on cities in *Tristes Tropiques* (1955). See Aldo Rossi, *The Architecture of the City*, trans Diane Ghirardo and Joan Ockman, The MIT Press (Cambridge, MA and London), 1984, pp 180–81.
2. Victor Hugo, *Notre-Dame de Paris*, trans John Sturrock, Penguin Classics (London), 1978.
3. Aldo Rossi, *A Scientific Autobiography*, The MIT Press (Cambridge MA & London) 1981.
4. *L'Eclisse*, directed by Michelangelo Antonioni, Cineriz (Rome), 1962.

Light and shadow are a key consideration in the design of the spaces at Walmer Yard, highlighting the sensuality and experience of the project.

# WORKING WITH ARCHITECTS

Peter Salter,
Walmer Yard,
London,
2016

Binet's photography of Walmer Yard also highlights the relationships between materials. Here, the concrete benches that sit around the perimeter of the courtyard are contrasted with the oak of the shutters and front doors.

The tightknit spaces of the four interlocking houses of Walmer Yard are captured in the photography of Hélène Binet. Their rooflines sit within the context of the surrounding homes of Notting Hill.

Externally at Walmer Yard, colours and textures contrast while sitting side by side. It is difficult to capture in a photograph, but here at the entrance to the four houses, Binet has picked up the red painted render and the grey of the staircase.

# FROM PROCESS TO IDENTITY

The small-scale London development and investment company Baylight Properties encourages a nimble spatial and material dialogue away from the normal slick representation of fait-accompli solutions. Its founder, architect **Crispin Kelly**, describes how this produces highly particular architecture born out of exploration and mutual respect – such as the extraordinary Walmer Yard.

As a small-scale developer and founder of Baylight Properties, I tend to commission smaller practices, working face-to-face with the people who started these firms and whose approach I admired from early on. Although there is no particular order of play, more often than not I first notice a practice not through its marketing or position in the media, but through its connection to a school of architecture, through 'crits', shows and lectures, in listening to the ways architects speak about their work. This is an engagement with education, a testament to a certain level of conscientiousness. For me the process is successful if, having learned something new, I feel driven to take out a pencil and write a note for myself.

This is the sort of communication that is enjoyable, and one weighted more towards earnestness – sincerity and authenticity – than marketing or branding. Particular architects might have a preoccupation with landscape, with the nuts and bolts of building construction or with formal invention. This is fundamental material about the make-up of a practice, and viewed through the lens of architecture schools it has an academic imprimatur. It is neither polished nor spun.

Walmer Yard, for example, is a small, innovative housing development that Baylight Properties commissioned in West London that came about through my being taught by its architect, Peter Salter, at the Architectural Association (AA). The houses now form the home of the Baylight Foundation, a charitable organisation with the aim of increasing public understanding of what architecture can do, rooted in the experience of Walmer Yard. *The Observer*'s architecture critic Rowan Moore described the way the houses might be experienced in his review of the buildings, writing: 'The project takes as far as it can the ideas that architecture might be sensual and bodily, and that its poetry lies in relationships between the minerals and spaces of buildings and the lives they contain.'[1] This sentiment is also present in Hélène Binet's photography of Walmer Yard. Her photographs are a continuation of the sort of considered or even searching communication I value.

Peter Salter,
Walmer Yard,
London,
2016

When working on Walmer Yard, Salter would design through drawings and models. This photograph shows one of the many models he made to explore the yurt spaces that sit at the top of each of the houses.

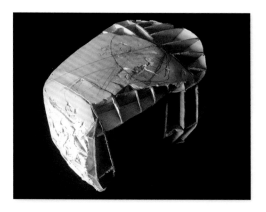

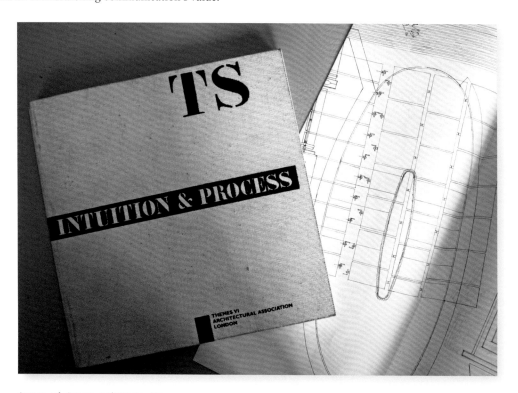

Cover of Peter Salter's *TS: Intuition & Process*, 1989

The *TS* series of publications was produced by the Architectural Association and accompanied an exhibition at the school. The book features projects selected from the Technical Studies unit Salter taught.

Sergison Bates,
Suburban Housing,
Aldershot,
Hampshire,
2016

Flyers and books were produced by Sergison
Bates for Baylight's 14-home scheme in Aldershot.
This flyer was designed specifically for a visit for
friends and colleagues, which Baylight arranges
once a project is complete.

# In making their case, invention, delight and conscientiousness need to be at architects' fingertips

Once Baylight Properties has engaged an architect for a project, the relationship becomes one of creative meetings with byways and alternatives explored. The process is linear, although research, precedents, constraints and opportunities are rehearsed. As they progress, proposals gather a sort of inevitable authority. Gathered into a form of brochure, the project is encapsulated, depicted and explained.

Printed paper becomes the medium for sketches, the development of ideas, the discussion of potential. Old-fashioned drawing is the life of this authentic communication, as are architectural models developed through the life of a project that offer a sense of immediacy derived from their having been put together in the studio. On the desk of a meeting room they can be questioned, manipulated and admired.

When a scheme is finally complete, we often arrange a visit for friends and colleagues to view and discuss it, as we did for the 14 houses we built in Aldershot with Sergison Bates. Flyers are produced for the day as short summaries describing the building. These events are an important part of the way Baylight Properties creates a culture around the work of the architects we collaborate with, and how we jointly communicate what we have set out to achieve.

Similarly, the materials architects offer clients should not be about slick presentation, but instead the creativity, nimbleness, concern, attention and anxiety that, evolving over time, enable a worthwhile project to satisfy three-dimensional life. In making their case, invention, delight and conscientiousness need to be at architects' fingertips. ⌀

**Note**

1. Rowan Moore, 'Walmer Yard Review – Uncompromising Beauty', *The Observer*, 20 November 2016: www.theguardian.com/artanddesign/2016/nov/20/walmer-yard-london-peter-salter-review

# Exhibiting Architecture

## Between the Profession and the Public

The Architect from 'Out of Character:
A Project by Studio MUTT',
Sir John Soane's Museum, London,
12 September – 18 November 2018

*opposite:* In 1812, John Soane wrote *Crude Hints towards
an History of my House*, in which he imagined his home
as a ruin centuries in the future, inspected by visitors who
speculate on its origins and function.

View from the Domed Area to the
Foyle Space from 'Out of Character:
A Project by Studio MUTT',
Sir John Soane's Museum, London,
12 September – 18 November 2018

*right:* Soane suggested that visitors might infer the
museum to have been inhabited by four characters,
which MUTT, a studio based in London and Liverpool,
brought to life over 200 years later as architectural
compositions of ornament, colour and form, speculating
on architecture's ability to communicate and carry
meaning.

London's Sir John Soane's Museum Senior Curator, **Owen Hopkins**, recounts the modern-day encumbrances and successes of communicating architecture to the public. This mission to attract the public's understanding and appreciation of architecture is crucial to giving people the 'tools' with which to discuss and debate architecture thoughtfully in all arenas of civic life.

Architecture is a slow business. It takes a long time to make a design, longer to build and that is before we even get to inhabitation and use. This aspect of architecture unfolds even more slowly, through multiple perspectives and dimensions and through our senses, cognition and memory. To understand a building is a complex process: some buildings we never understand; and even the simplest, most straightforward contains far more than can be represented via some carefully staged photographs and a few lines of copy lifted from a press release, or worse, from what catches our eye scrolling through Instagram. Yet, with the decline of the architectural press, and with architecture now almost invisible in the general media, this has become the typical source material through which we are reduced to trying to understand much of the architecture that is produced today.

There are, of course, several upsides to this transformation: the mass of information presented to us by online blogs, magazines and social media exposes us to buildings and architects that we would never have encountered before, and there is certainly nothing wrong with any of these platforms in and of themselves. The issue is that while there is still great architectural journalism and criticism happening, it struggles to get through the online deluge and receive the attention or influence it used to have. In addition, unless one is in possession of one of the very few salaried jobs now on offer, it is simply impossible to make a living these days writing about architecture. The result is that it has become either a labour of love, accessible only to the privileged few lucky enough to have other sources of income, or is left to the dwindling number of journalists working on a treadmill of X articles per day, with predictable and understandable results in terms of the quality of what is written.

*… of Decoration* from 'Origins – A Project by Ordinary Architecture', Royal Academy of Arts, London, 15 October 2016 – 15 January 2017

In 2016 and 2017 a number of the artworks usually installed in the buildings of the Royal Academy of Arts in London were temporarily removed as building work took place. This provided the opportunity to commission a project by London firm Ordinary Architecture.

## Culture and Curating

Given present trends, it is hard to see how this situation is going to change. Yet it is far from the case that the architectural culture that existed in the written word has disappeared – it has simply jumped medium. As architectural writing has declined in prominence, we have seen an explosion in the numbers of architecture exhibitions, displays, installations, biennales, events and discussions of all types. While much of this has issued from professional spheres, significantly there are now a number of museums and cultural institutions that have well-established architectural departments, with the institutional backing and resources to do significant work. One of the interesting results of these two parallel phenomena is that many curatorial positions dedicated to architecture or related fields are now occupied by former journalists. However, for those working in the context of a museum – the particular focus of this article – the audience they address is fundamentally different.

Much of the architectural 'curating' – and the popularisation of the practice, as well as title, means it applies to a broad spectrum of activity – is, of course, still aimed at the profession or those with a specialist interest. This is much the same audience segment as for the trade press and its online successors, even as the internet has seen it grow in scale and become much more international. The audience of museums, in contrast, is mostly unspecialised and also rather more local. Even if every one of the 22,000 or so people who work in the architecture sector in London visited an architecture exhibition, all but the most modest of shows would still struggle to break even.[1] As a result, curators of architecture working in a museum context have both the challenge and privilege of speaking directly to the public, thereby playing a vital role as interface, interlocutor and arbiter between the profession and the world outside.

## Exhibitions as Architecture

One of the consequences of the new prominence of architecture curating, both within and outside the context of museums, is the emergence of new approaches to the staging of architecture exhibitions. Gone are the days of exhibitions of architecture simply being displays of drawings and models, presented dryly as stand-ins for the unavoidably absent building(s). Instead, there is a growing trend of the 'exhibition as architecture': that is, the thing being exhibited actually constitutes a work of architecture. We see this manifested in the pavilions, structures and installations that have become such a familiar feature of architectural culture, which unlike traditional architecture exhibitions and whether their curators realise it or not, constitute a concerted attempt to break down the practical and conceptual barriers between architecture and its display. Taking representation out of the equation, the exhibition itself becomes architecture.

The most obvious precedents of this phenomenon are the buildings and structures created for World's Fairs and Expos, and looking further back, the literal pavilion or garden folly. However, the forces driving the trend of 'exhibition as architecture', when it comes to museums or other equivalent cultural institutions, are, I would argue, also particular to the contexts in which those projects take place. In large cultural institutions which have a focus beyond architecture, curators often find themselves having to fight their corner, arguing against the perception that their subject is highly specialist, difficult for a broad public audience to understand, and creatively and financially risky, particularly in the ancillary parts of the organisation (marketing, press, fundraising, commercial, etc). Thus, for curators of architecture working in institutional settings who have to justify the popular appeal of their projects, the success of immersive and experiential programmes in other areas of culture – from Tate Modern's Turbine Hall to Secret Cinema – present a ready and highly relatable model. Part of the appeal of these projects, especially with regard to somewhere like the Turbine Hall, is closely related to architectural concerns: many are spatial propositions, which depend on the publicness of the spaces they occupy. When it comes to galleries and museum spaces, this publicness also goes hand in hand with a rarefied status and certain codes of behaviour, and it is clear that part of the appeal of these types of immersive and experiential projects is to do with their playful subversion of the spaces they occupy.

If the curator-turned-commissioner of a pavilion, installation, structure etc is to some degree a reflection of the institutional contexts in which he or she operates, the phenomenon, and in particular the fact that there is no shortage of architects looking for such an opportunity, is also partly attributable to changes internal to the profession and the ways architects are more typically commissioned. Gone are the days of Leicester University's Engineering Building (James Gowan and James Stirling, commissioned 1957) or Paris's Pompidou Centre (Richard Rogers, Renzo Piano and Gianfranco Franchini, commissioned 1971) where clients would take a risk on young, untested architects with radical ideas. As a result these types of 'cultural commission' have become an important way for young architects to build, test ideas and gain publicity for their work. But these opportunities are not just confined to young architects. That London's Serpentine Gallery has, even with the stipulation that architects of its annual pavilion cannot have built in the UK before, been able to roll out such a roster of global stars to design it, is surely a reflection of a commissioning culture and regulatory systems that guard against the overtly risky or experimental.

*… of Construction* from 'Origins –
A Project by Ordinary Architecture',
Royal Academy of Arts, London,
15 October 2016 – 15 January 2017

Comprising a series of interventions around the building, *Origins* asked visitors to look again at the myths, conventions and histories that guide how architecture is created and experienced in ways that were playful, witty and provocative.

These types of 'cultural commission' have become an important way for young architects to build, test ideas and gain publicity for their work

*… of Space* from 'Origins –
A Project by Ordinary Architecture',
Royal Academy of Arts, London,
15 October 2016 – 15 January 2017

The history of architecture is full of 'origin myths': stories of how and where architecture began. The brief put to Ordinary Architecture was to explore these 'origin myths' and create a provocative allegory of the foundations of contemporary architecture.

Front Kitchen installation from
'Adam Nathaniel Furman: The Roman Singularity',
Sir John Soane's Museum, London,
16 September – 10 December 2017

Installed in the recently restored Kitchens at Sir John Soane's Museum, this project comprised an imaginary Roman city of colourful, 3D-printed ceramic models, drawings and a 'video-poem', all of which Furman created while resident at the British School at Rome.

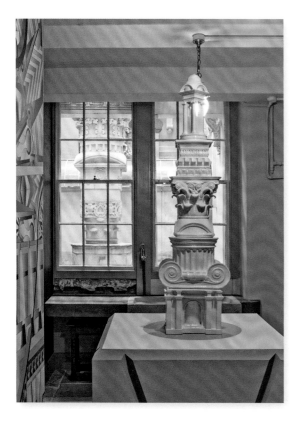

*Pasteeshio* from 'Adam Nathaniel Furman:
The Roman Singularity',
Sir John Soane's Museum, London,
16 September – 10 December 2017

For the project, Furman also created two new Soane-inspired works: *Pasteeshio*, which remixes historical forms in a single structure that combines new technological capabilities with traditional craft; and *Capreeshio*, which abstracts these forms into a mural world of patterns.

## Impacts and Effects

In trying to assess the impact of the 'exhibition as architecture', there are a number of obvious positives that come straight into view: opening up architecture to new audiences; a democratisation of experience, with all responses equally valid; opportunities for young practices to gain exposure working for prestigious clients; and the chance to reacquaint ourselves with the sensory, as opposed to imagistic, aspects of architecture. Yet, at the same time, we must also be mindful and attuned towards the effects, implications and potential downsides of this phenomenon.

Firstly, the focus on the 'authentic' experience of the original belies a rather conservative notion of architecture that, in place of valuing the image, fetishises the aura of the building-as-object, whose power, in Walter Benjamin's famous words, rests upon 'Its presence in time and space, its unique existence at the place where it happens to be'.[2] In that same essay, Benjamin predicted that the mechanical reproduction of images would undermine the aura of the original work of art. However, in the digital age, precisely the opposite has occurred. The reproduction of images of an object has arguably led to its aura only becoming stronger. Less abstractly, we see this in the trend now towards exhibitions that are Instagram friendly, as a way of driving interest and ultimately visits. It is not simply that objects are selected with a view to the reproducibility of their image, but that this is beginning to inform the practice of design itself.

There is nothing inherently bad about the ability of architecture to be made into an image. And there is no reason why an Instagram-friendly design might not also be interesting in its own right. There are clearly great rewards on offer for those who are able to strike this balance. Yet for every young architect who gets commissioned by a museum or cultural institution, it is inevitable that there are many orders of magnitude more who do not. As a result, curators have a huge responsibility in making sure they pick the right winners. It is not like the art world, where exhibitions are the main sphere in which artists operate (and compete). For architects, working on an exhibition or cultural commission is a quite distinct sphere of production, one that is separate from the profession, where the normal rules do not apply: the young and untested are able to compete with the famous and established, and many of the usual constraints of brief in terms of planning regulations, experimentation or even function work quite differently. Consequently it is not simply a question of whether a curator picks the right 'winners'; on a structural level the very image of architecture this type of curatorial practice portrays to the public is an inherently distorted one.

Egg from Terry Farrell's TV-am building, London, 1982, from 'The Return of the Past: Postmodernism in British Architecture', Sir John Soane's Museum, London, 16 May – 27 August 2018

Bringing together a range of projects associated with Postmodernism in British architecture, one of the key strategies of this project was to situate objects in the historic Soane interiors with the explicit intention of forming new connections, new resonances and ultimately new meanings.

South Drawing Room from 'The Return of the Past: Postmodernism in British Architecture', Sir John Soane's Museum, London, 16 May – 27 August 2018

Here, a Terry Farrell chair from the TV-am building is positioned alongside Soane's own sofa. In this way the meaning issues not just from the intervention or the setting, but their interrelation and the collision of different contexts.

## Critical Practice

So where does this leave the practice of 'curating architecture', especially in the context of museums? It is clearly positive that more institutions are taking architecture seriously, and that curators have agency to explore their subject in multiple disciplines and dimensions. This is all the more important given the way 'curating' has been appropriated and as a label applied to activities that have little or no intellectual basis or endeavour. The vital thing, however, is for curators working in museums to be acutely aware of the contexts in which they operate, and in doing so to ensure that their curatorial practice is also a critical practice. If there are distortions inherent, for example, in the exhibition as a framework for the presentation of ideas then curators must find ways to break them down – and in this, the very notion of the 'exhibition as architecture' offers a clue.

One of the interesting and useful effects of the prevalence of these types of projects and kinds of approach has been to remind us that all architecture is ultimately on display. Every building we see and experience in our daily lives is on display in some way as a work of architecture. We may not perceive it as such, because there is no banner saying 'exhibition' or surrounding cultural apparatus, but we can, if we want to, conceive and experience it the same way we do a pavilion, installation or structure. I believe one of the important aspects to the role of curator of architecture is not just to mount projects and create interesting commissions, but to try to *dissolve* the distinction between architecture that is created purely to be displayed and architecture that is not – which after all is actually the architecture that matters most. When we put architecture on display it needs to exist in a context that is not purely cultural: it has to exist in the real world.

And this task is an important and urgent one. The future of cities depends on their inhabitants being able to see how architecture is made, and having a sense of the forces that shape it for good and for ill. Everyone is curious about a new building going up, but few are really able to comprehend it. People want the tools to understand their built environments. It is our job as curators to look beyond the deluge of information and images and find ways to make those tools available to all. ⌂

**Notes**
1. Mark Wingham, *London's Architectural Sector: Working Paper 86*, Greater London Authority (London), March 2017: www.london.gov.uk/sites/default/files/architecture_paper_wp86.pdf.
2. Walter Benjamin, 'The Work of Art in the Age of Mechanical Reproduction', in Walter Benjamin, *Illuminations*, edited by Hannah Arendt, Pimlico (London), 1999, p 214.

Exhibition Gallery from 'The Return of the Past: Postmodernism in British Architecture', Sir John Soane's Museum, London, 16 May – 27 August 2018

The exhibition was conceived in two parts: interventions in the Soane interiors, and here, in the Exhibition Galleries where historic interiors act as interventions in the exhibition. Central to the approach was playing with colour and material, including the creation of a new carpet.

# TEST

**Roger Howie**

# COMMUNICATION THROUGH

# BED

Zaha Hadid Design,
Braid vases and
candleholders,
2016

The Braid collection has evolved
from Zaha Hadid Architects'
ongoing research and studies into
the formal language of towers.

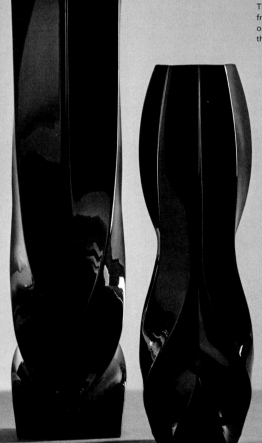

PRODUCT DESIGN

Zaha Hadid Architects has become a global brand designing not only breathtaking buildings but also shoes, chairs, jewellery and tables, amongst other things. **Roger Howie** has been leading public relations for this maelstrom of creativity since 2004, and here describes how the practice applies its design ethos equally to these items as it does to architecture.

Zaha Hadid Design,
Nova shoe for United Nude,
2013

To achieve the shoe's seamless detailing, ZHD collaborated with United Nude to invent a new method of shoemaking involving rotation moulding (the first time ever used to create a shoe) combined with injection moulding and hand-moulded techniques such as vacuum casting.

From the very beginnings of the practice in 1979, Zaha Hadid Architects (ZHA) has explored and expressed the formal, structural and material strategies within its architecture through product designs. Zaha Hadid Design (ZHD) was established in 2006 to collaborate with a diversity of industries, researching and developing new methods and technologies for product, furniture and fashion design. Adopting an architectural approach (where a complex brief incorporating numerous criteria including programme, context, budget, timescale, as well as the interests of all stakeholders defines the design's core principles), ZHD's formal determinations for products stem from this logical assimilation of constraints to establish a set of rules that are used to test ideas and concepts in an iterative process of experimentation and development.

### Continuing a Mathematic Process

These product designs continue Zaha Hadid's strong affinity with mathematics, which is embedded within the DNA of the studio's methodology and process. Multifaceted puzzles are solved by establishing a ruleset and developing formulae to find not only obvious solutions, but also to question and push the boundaries of what is possible – from the subtle to the extreme – while still meeting all defined criteria, often achieving the unexpected solutions that have come to define ZHA's repertoire.

Zaha Hadid Design,
Pelago table for Citco,
2019

Referencing rock formations carved and smoothed by the sea, the Pelago coffee table conveys the studio's interest in natural systems. Comprising two interlocking, contrasting elements of black marble and transparent acrylic, the table's horizontal surface appears fluid, the concentric waves milled within the acrylic adding depth and complexity through refraction.

Zaha Hadid Design,
Mesa table for Vitra,
2007

Evolving from ZHA's architectural
experiment (*Elastika* installation, Miami,
2005) to create connections in which an
organic set of tentacles linked spaces
and floors across the atrium, the Mesa
Table continued this research of form
and space interwoven with structure.

Zaha Hadid Design,
Ultrastellar chairs for
David Gill Gallery,
London,
2019

Working in traditional materials of walnut and
leather, the Ultrastellar chairs continue the
studio's exploration of the complex curvilinear
forms and structures within nature.

This process places ZHD's designs within an architectural perspective where furniture, products and even jewellery communicate the studio's research into new spatial and formal ideas, materials and manufacturing technologies in architecture. Describing the Mesa table for Vitra (2007), Edwin Heathcote explained: 'Mesa becomes a microcosmic extrusion of the spatial ideas inherent in Zaha's architecture. Form doesn't follow only function but instead is drawn along by the flow of space.'[1]

## Digital Design and Fabrication

Creating new design tools to generate geometries shaped by functional considerations, structural performance and material utilisation, the studio's product designs also combine new digital design with the skills of traditional manufacture and craftsmanship. The B.zero1 collection of jewellery for Bulgari (2016 and 2018) evolved from a set of principles established by ZHD to address a variety of criteria including: predetermined dimensions that incorporate a flat surface for the engraved BVLGARI motif; the volume of gold within each piece; and working to a degree of detail and resolution that exhibits the expertise of Bulgari's jewellers who create each piece by hand. These core principles, in conjunction with the material performances of gold, set the geometric constraints of the collection.

Displaying a collective, multidisciplinary approach to problem solving, the studio's product designs thus communicate a detailed understanding of new digital design and fabrication technologies. For the Nova shoe (2013), ZHD collaborated with the manufacturer United Nude to engineer a new method of shoemaking. Injection and rotation moulding together with vacuum casting were employed to create the seamless upper. Striations juxtaposed with realignments express the shoe's primary structure, which incorporates a cantilevered system that allows the 16-centimetre (6.25-inch) heel to appear unsupported.

The Ultrastellar chairs in walnut for the David Gill Gallery in London (2016) demonstrate the exchange of structural forces with a sculptural sensibility derived from ZHD's ongoing explorations of the relationships between structure and surface. These same digital investigations have enabled the iterative development of, and are clearly evident within, each of the practice's architectural projects.

As Joseph Giovannini has summarised: 'For Le Corbusier, the plan was the generator, but for ZHA, three-dimensions, stereometric rather than planimetric, is the generator of designs conceived simultaneously as plan, section, and elevation.'[2] ⊿

Zaha Hadid Design,
B.zero1 ring for Bulgari,
2016

Bulgari's original B.zero1 ring (1999) was inspired by the Colosseum. Zaha Hadid Design reinterpreted this concept in 2016, addressing a set of predetermined constraints and material considerations that defined the ring's geometric composition.

Notes
1. Edwin Heathcote, 'Mesa by Zaha Hadid', *Dezeen*, 6 June 2007: www.dezeen.com/2007/06/06/mesa-by-zaha-hadid/.
2. Joseph Giovannini, 'Fast Forward', *Heydar Aliyev Centre (Design)*, Lars Müller (Zurich), 2013, p 33.

# THE SOCIAL MEDIA MONSTER

London-based designer and architectural tutor **Adam Nathaniel Furman** has built a large number of followers on social media platforms such as Instagram. As well as using this to publish his work, awards, students' work and the buildings he admires, he also uses it for more polemic effect, such as exposing those architects who have unpaid interns or attacking the politics of neoliberalism.

# Dangers and Thrills Only Partially Glimpsed

Metahaven,
sprawl.space website,
2016

Made by Metahaven as a snapshot of the 2015 film project *The Sprawl (Propaganda about Propaganda)*, the website shows the intense and jarring recompositions of familiar internet media and tropes that they deploy with fragments of text and news media, to render our experience of the web thoroughly uncanny and reveal its fundamental structures.

Rem Koolhaas→

popular baby meme→

Adam Nathaniel Furman,
Collage created for Tumblr,
2011

The collage, which also exists in animated GIF format, is an evocative compression of multiple issues and themes of the time related to the speeding up of culture and politics through the infiltration of the internet into everyday life.

We are living through a period of massive tectonic alignment in terms of who controls the information and media people consume. Until recently this information was in the hands of governments, a cadre of institutionally anointed experts and a very small group of oligarchic magnates. Now, it is suddenly open and up for grabs. Within this state of digital chaos, the most intellectually and technically nimble are able to shape spaces in which they can project values they wish to proselytise, even though – and as if counterintuitively – this tumultuous and riven landscape has been created and fostered on platforms owned by some of the biggest corporations in capitalist history. While the traditional media act as a counterweight, they are increasingly portrayed as a relic yet to be swept aside by the all-engulfing digital storm.

Architecture as a field of communication and discourse is an island of impressively stubborn, actively reinforced anachronisms within an otherwise radical and unrecognisable environment. After a brief efflorescence of attenuated discussions on Twitter, and – prior to that – some thoughtful output on blogging platforms, 'gatekeeping' has returned with a vengeance. Meanwhile a plethora of small publications and a range of major international newspapers with correspondents has imploded into the seemingly unstoppable and, in my view, editorially opaque media singularity that is *Dezeen* while a handful of major-outlet correspondents remain attractive to their employers through sensationalising mainstream content.

Andreas Angelidakis,
*Commonwealth*,
2018

A collage exploring the power of meme-like overlays of image and text.

Considering architecture has a history of being at the forefront of technological and cultural change, it is strange to find that within this broader context of fragmentation, the profession seems to view social media as, more or less, either a funny thing hipsters use to share images of their avocado-toast or simply as a free form of traditional advertising. Almost uniformly, architects seem to miss both its danger and its excitement, regressing to the comfortable formats of magazines and journals – back, that is, to a near-Luddite fetishisation of the printed object and, in doing so, eschewing creative or critical engagement with the very technologies that are creating and accelerating the ruptures in the world around them.

### Embarrassing Dads of the Internet

It is in this context that a steady and deathly drip of digital posts by once radical practices is so very hard to digest. How sorry it is to see practices using this medium to say little more than that they are 'so proud to announce that', 'so honoured', 'excited to be completing', 'thrilled to have won' or even 'so proud of our team's charity fund-raising bake sale'. The worst must surely be 'welcome to Cannes after an epic bike ride!' accompanied by magazine-like images of ersatz 'friends together' or iPhone selfies or painfully nostalgic collage-like faux-handmade renders harking back to some illusory pre-digital golden age.

officialnormanfoster • Following

officialnormanfoster Time for the unicorn .
Load more comments

jasperfab Norman Foster is my spirit animal 🖤

sol_cucuruc @akimovadesign 🔯

tayprate Love love love

Liked by ginexmarco and 30,630 others

JULY 28, 2018

Add a comment...

Norman Foster on an inflatable unicorn, 2018

A widely circulated image posted on Norman Foster's official Instagram account, 28 July 2018, that became an internet sensation in architectural circles.

This landscape of architectural mediation is so featureless and devoid of spunk that Norman Foster posting an image of himself on an inflatable unicorn in a swimming pool was pretty much the most exciting event to have happened on any of the major platforms in 2018, while the publication of *Archigram: The Book* was such a widely discussed event partly because Archigram represents the last time – *fifty years ago!* – architects were successful in co-opting and instrumentalising new forms of mediation with any gusto.[1] One of the few critics who have used the new media in a thrillingly non-traditional manner is Kate Wagner, aka @mcmansionhell, whose direct and visceral passion has garnered 45,000 followers on Twitter alone.

Kate Wagner,
@McMansionHell Twitter profile header,
29 January 2019

An illustration of the direct, forceful and often humorous
manner in which Wagner relates to her followers through
the limitations of the social media she deploys.

Kate Wagner,
Meme from McMansion Hell
blog,
6 November 2018

An example of how Wagner uses architecture
and memes to make broader political points.

Metahaven, a Dutch collective, have been operating freely across politics,
international relations, graphic design, fine art, video, web design, architecture,
history and speculative fiction since the early 2000s. Their work uncovers strange
truths and moments of exception that reveal much about the nature of this new
world we inhabit, as well as the terrifying centralisation of Web 2.0, in which we
operate entirely within ecosystems driven from Palo Alto, Cupertino and Seattle,
and which, bizarrely, are surreptitiously manipulated from Moscow, Macedonia,
Tehran and Tel Aviv. Certain members of the architectural avant-garde justify
a retreat to the printed page through critiques of a corporatised internet, yet
Metahaven show how one can operate within it both critically and reflexively.
They actively harness the aesthetics of both the various web-based subcultures
that have bloomed online over the past decade and the visual language of the
banal platforms themselves, transforming these into shocking new formulations
of image, text and narrative that reveal the latent political ideologies at work
behind what most of us presume to be neutral material. Metahaven are very
much creatures of this new media-technological ecosystem, and it is precisely
their acquaintance with it that allows them to be so fascinatingly critical of it.

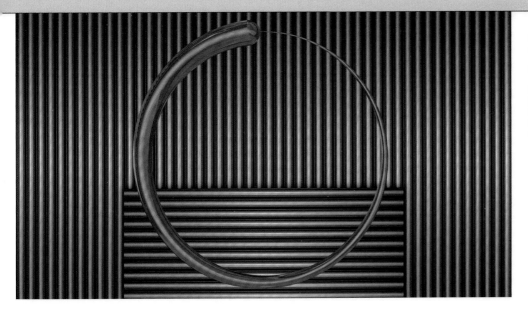

Metahaven,
*Eurasia
(Questions on Happiness),*
2018

*left and opposite bottom:* Screenshots from the video illustrating how Metahaven critically refashion the aesthetics of the internet into strange new formats and combinations.

The modes of mediated engagement of both Wagner and Metahaven offer intriguing and potentially unsettling ways of cutting through the turgid sedimentation of architectural discourse in communicating clear, consistent and relevant messages about the meaning of architecture in a broader cultural and political context. This is the *authenticity imperative*, a crucial factor in harnessing and directing the energies of observers who become, rather than followers, potent and passionate believers in an entire perspective on the world and the profession. Digital platforms have also re-empowered the art of rhetoric, the modulation of speech for emotive effect that can catch the attention of a population weary of manipulation and bored of pre-packaged corporate guff.

## Children of the Internet

Like Wagner and Metahaven, the millennial generation has grown up with the internet. As it has mutated through various incarnations, many of us have pursued the evolving ways in which we can reach audiences, from Geocities and Tripod sites in the 1990s, to web forums, blogs, standard websites, Facebook groups, Tumblr and eventually other social media and Instagram, all the while producing work, in text, images, animations, videos and drawings operating effectively on each of these various platforms.

Participation in an ever-shifting online culture has profoundly affected the development of those of us who were active at each of its stages and platforms. Our thinking, sensibility and general political and aesthetic awareness became fundamentally linked to the plurality of our online experiences, inculcating us with a dynamic and promiscuous relationship to a diverse array of media, content and modes of representation.

Having experienced this fluid and engaging world, it was – to say the least – quite a shock for architecture students and young practitioners to find themselves in institutions and studios struggling to digest the consequences of the early 1990s pre-internet-era digital revolution, let alone creatively engaging with the landscape of a world so saturated in mediation and digital exchange that its occupants are virtually cyborgs.

When it came to aesthetics, the situation seemed even more comical, with architects fussing over a palette of formal interests so limited and narrow that Postmodernism – a short-lived and really rather tame opening-up of the architectural canon – would send them into paroxysms of disgust. It was impossible to square this with the coruscating, cascading, bewildering and utterly vibrant array of aesthetic and communicative approaches developing in the world around this closed time-capsule coffin of architectural practice.

Critical memes from the AdamNathanielFurman Instagram account, 2018–19

A small selection of critical memes created by the author, which are often accompanied by texts elaborating the point.

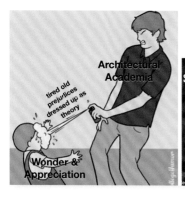

## Rebelling Against the Algorithm

Messier and less refined than either Wagner or Metahaven, my own online engagement has attempted to harness the various media I have had the pleasure of learning and using over the years as well as the taste cultures I have been a part of and moved through with the goal of breaking down preconceptions and rigid value judgements of the architectural mainstream – from long-form visual-video-lectures, to animated GIFs, to what has come to be a most useful and potent fulcrum, Instagram.

Perhaps the final apotheosis and most addictive incarnation of the Web 2.0 platforms, Instagram lends itself perfectly to architecture in terms of the primacy it affords the image. Architects tend to 'stay on message' and stick to one type of content online, but I have found the opposite tactic has been far more fruitful in terms of treating my feed as a fulfilling research project in its own right.

There are several different threads of content that I constantly jump between, bamboozling the Instagram algorithm – which promotes consistency – in the process. The main body of my posts addresses the notion of alternative histories and celebrates the sheer diversity and range of buildings, architectures, modes of living, aesthetics and taste-cultures which exist and have existed in the world, and which have been excluded from the architectural canon and its textbooks. Then there are the posts which test and question the boundaries of good taste and orthodox value, pushing the observer to question why they consider certain things good, and others bad, by posting examples which might initially revile, but on closer inspection should reveal a great deal of interest – a celebration of the ugly and the camp, as it were. I also regularly create polemical posts under the hashtag #archiphorisms that come in two types. On the one hand there are meme-like critical statements that operate through humour, and the mixing of image and text, and on the other, there are billboard-style textual posts that are effectively little cannonballs of theory, fragments and aphorisms that hit the ground and stir up conversation and debate. These relate to general contemporary issues or to articles published in the design world, deconstructing them from a particular – and usually progressive – standpoint. Finally, there are the poetic posts, cryptic

**A TV SHOW IN WHICH ALL THE RESIDENTS OF POUNDBURY SWAP HOMES WITH ALL THE RESIDENTS OF THE BARBICAN FOR A MONTH AND REALISE THAT ITS ALL JUST DIFFERENT WINDOW DRESSING ON THE SAME FUNDAMENTALLY ROTTEN MIDDLE CLASS ENGLISHNESS**

Critical-poetic meme from the AdamNathanielFurman Instagram account,
29 January 2019

An example of the kind of memes in which the author explores attitudes, value judgements and preconceptions through miniature scenarios and poetic vignettes.

but expansive moments of visual or textual reprieve that force a hint of enigma into what is otherwise a very direct stream of unambiguously delivered material. The stream is delivered with a forceful voice, which throws in quite a lot of personal detail in a manner that might be taken as 'oversharing', yet this blows away any idea that it might be compared to the majority of architecture accounts that stick carefully to a narrow message of product-promotion. Instead, this is an attempt to convey an entire mode-of-being that can be bought into, rejected forcefully or observed with curiosity, one that spans aesthetics, architecture, politics, design and art, and which extends outwards to other platforms. It also incorporates a strong vector of self-promotion that has led to a slew of highly productive opportunities in academia and design.

## On to the Next Paradigm

As Web 2.0 is reaching full maturity, and will no doubt soon come to the end of its period of dominance, architecture has still barely begun to harness its potential. It would be highly beneficial for the vigour of the discipline if more of those who consider themselves to be progressive, peripheral, critical, or who simply have a lot of fire in their bellies, would leave their Luddite snobbery behind and pick up these weapons and tools of mass dissemination, deploying them in ways that can crack open the otherwise narrow range of interests and accepted approaches sanctified by the old gatekeepers of aesthetic decorum. As this 'new' media reaches its apogee and goes into decline, something new is coming; nobody knows what, yet whatever it may be, I very much hope that Generation Z will cast aside the architectural tendency to regress into materialist nostalgia, and take up whatever challenges and opportunities come in the world of mediation and intangible exchange with a confidence and exuberance befitting the field's somewhat obscured tradition of hyper-engagement with the contemporary world. ᗪ

**Note**
1. Dennis Crompton (ed), *Archigram: The Book*, Circa Press (London), 2018.

# China's Global Introspection

# Managing Critical Thinking

**Austin Williams**

**Austin Williams**, architect, course leader at London's Kingston University and expert correspondent on contemporary China's architecture scene, presents a brief vignette of architectural culture behind the Chinese firewall and the particular issues that affect it.

Jiakun Architects,
Tea House,
Jinhua Architecture Park,
Jinhua,
Zhejiang province,
2004

Jiakun was one of a number of architects chosen by Ai Wei Wei, from China and around the world, to design a series of pavilions on a long thin strip of land along the banks of the river Yiwu in Jinhua.

After Chairman Mao's death in 1976, China's universities began to admit a new generation – and a lost generation – of students, many of whom had their ambitions thwarted by the Cultural Revolution a few years earlier. Under the Maoist education policies of the early 1970s, university admission had been reserved for selected party loyalists and Stakhanovite-model workers who were simply nominated for a place regardless of intellectual merit. Indeed, in 1975, Deng Xiaoping noted that graduates were 'not even capable of reading a book',[1] while many of the best of the rest were sent down to the countryside to take up manual labour. In 1977, Deng introduced the first entrance examination since 1965, and opened the door for nearly 5.7 million students to compete for just 273,000 places.[2]

### The 'Experimental' Set

Pragmatism dictated that engineering was, for many, the university subject of choice: an essential building block for an emerging liberalised market economy. The Politburo was still almost exclusively made up of engineering graduates, and the original eight architecture schools – still highly regarded today – had names like the Harbin Institute of Building Technology, and Xi'an Institute of Metallurgical Building Engineering. But once the ban on studying the humanities was lifted, a modicum of design flair began to sneak into the construction market, and the first private architectural practice for 40 years, Atelier FCJZ, was founded in 1993–4.[3] Five years later, architects like Wang Shu, Liu Xiaodu, Dong Yugan and Ma Yansong were being hailed as the new Chinese avant-garde – the so-called 'experimental' set.[4]

Tong Ming Studio,
Zhou Chunya Art Studio,
Jiading,
Shanghai,
2008

The modern concrete form was introduced into the suburban district of Jiading to help celebrated artists set up residence in the rural economy.

Tong Ming Studio,
Dong's House and Restaurant,
Pingjian District,
Suzhou,
Jiangsu province,
2004

Suzhou is a UNESCO heritage city and careful restoration of this traditional courtyard house was essential along one of the city's most historic streets. The design is a harmonious balance: a contemporary aesthetic that retains a continuity with the past.

Those experiments continue, with thousands of architecture students graduating from flamboyant universities and practices in the West only to find their much-fêted creativity restricted somewhat when they return home. The sociopolitical environment required for genuine critical thinking does not yet exist in a sufficiently unfettered way back in China. This is not to say that Chinese in general, and Chinese architects in particular, are incapable of critical thought. Far from it. There is possibly a more pronounced willingness to experiment than in the West; it is just that efforts to stimulate creativity are quickly diluted by everyday social realities. 'Critical thinking entails questioning authority, and a certain degree of freedom of thought',[5] and for now that is not really acceptable. China both needs, and frowns upon, social disruptors.

Jiakun Architects,
West Village,
Chengdu,
Sichuan province,
2015

The spatial design of this commercial and leisure complex in the heart of the city allows locals to refresh their collective memories of a traditional leisurely lifestyle; strolling along the rooftops or sitting in the bamboo shade.

Wang Wei / Field Architecture Office,
Commercial building,
Panchenggang District,
Chengdu, Sichuan province,
2016

This city complex on an old industrial site is a striking urban intervention, but also a machine-aesthetic reference to those industrial jobs lost over the years. The project celebrates the diversity of Chengdu's migrant population.

## Informal Mechanisms

It is hard to promote yourself and keep your head down at the same time. Architects like MAD, Urbanus and Neri&Hu are successful outward-facing practices with an international profile, but not even Pritzker Prize-winner Wang Shu feels it is necessary to have a website. For many architects in China, Chinese commissions come through reputation, acceptance and networking that establishes 'long lasting institutional connections … (and) informal mechanisms.'[6] As a result, many often find themselves hostage to the government's whims, policy objectives or inducements. In this respect, the idea of promoting oneself on the open market is often available only to those with other forms of income. For example, China's 'experimental architects are also teachers at local universities' and are promoted via academic journals like *Time + Architecture*.[7]

In the most rapidly urbanising country in the world, when official policy dictates that the countryside is the new big idea, many Chinese architects nod sagely. It is a situation that leads to centripetal creativity: a desire to look outwards while being pulled ever inwards. A desire for autonomy while dependent on others. This is not a particularly healthy creative environment, but for some these very tensions spark more innovative architectural responses and are helping to forge a quietly defiant new Chinese architecture. ᴆ

# Tensions spark more innovative architectural responses and are helping to forge a quietly defiant new Chinese architecture

### Notes
1. Frederica M Bunge and Rinn-Sup Shinn, *China: A Country Study*, Foreign Area Studies, The American University (Washington DC), 1980, p 148.
2. Weihua Liu, *The Struggles of an Ordinary Man: The Turbulent History of China Through a Farmer's Eyes from 1900 to 2000*, vol 2, Lulu.com (Raleigh, NC), 2017, p 506.
3. Jianfei Zhu, 'Criticality in Between China and the West', *Journal of Architecture*, 10 (5), November 2005, pp 479–98.
4. Ding Guanghui, 'Experimental Architecture in China', *Journal of the Society of Architectural Historians*, 73 (1), 2014, pp 28–37.
5. Rosaline May Lee and Yanyue Yuan, 'Innovation Education in China: Preparing Attitudes, Approaches, and Intellectual Environments for Life in the Automation Economy', in Nancy W Gleason (ed), *Higher Education in the Era of the Fourth Industrial Revolution*, Springer (Singapore), 2018, pp 93–119.
6. Ettore Santi, 'Uncertainty and Design Practice in China: The "Apparatus" of Shanghai Experimental Architecture', *Journal of Architecture and Urbanism*, 41 (2), 2017, pp 120–8.
7. *Ibid.*

Wang Wei / Field Architecture Office,
Baima Village regeneration,
Sichuan province,
2016

The project traces regional Chinese architectural precedents. Each building expresses a lifestyle distinct from the city, designed in consultation with villagers and local craftspeople.

Justine Harvey

# New Architecture of the South Pacific

## How the Māori Worldview is Changing New Zealand's Built Environment

Monk Mackenzie with Novare,
Tūranganui Bridge,
Tūranganui a Kiwa,
Gisborne,
New Zealand,
2016

*opposite:* Competition-winning design for the Tūranganui Bridge in Gisborne, which connects the mainland to Te Taio A Taiau/Taiao, a historic rock in the Tūranganui River where, in 1769, British explorer Captain James Cook first made contact with the local Māori *iwi* (tribe).

Monk Mackenzie,
Foodstuffs Headquarters,
Auckland Airport,
due for completion late 2020

*above:* The architectural concept is sensitive to acknowledging the coastal landscape and basalt rock garden mounds formed by ancestors of the Māori people of Waiohua, which are still present at the Ōtuataua Stone Fields. Both the form of the building and the material palette draw reference from this volcanic landscape and its history as a significant place of food production.

Auckland-based architectural design writer **Justine Harvey** documents a new phenomenon in New Zealand's architectural community: an imperative that focuses on reflecting the Māori sensibility. This embodies respect for the land and a generous approach to interaction – giving and not taking, architecturally and socially.

New Zealand, or Aotearoa (its Māori name) has been learning important lessons in terms of developing a national identity through architecture that could make an important contribution to overseas architectural thinking, particularly within the former colonies and our increasingly diverse communities worldwide. Being a relatively young country, it has adopted Western styles of architecture since colonisation, formalised by the signing of the Treaty of Waitangi in 1840 by the British Crown and at least 500 Māori chiefs. It has only been since the mid-20th century that New Zealand's evolving identity started to be communicated through its architecture. In 1946, young Kiwi practice Group Architects said: 'Overseas solutions will not do. New Zealand must have its own architecture, its own sense of what is beautiful and appropriate to our climate and conditions.'[1] However, it has really only been in the past decade that New Zealand's indigenous history, culture and identity has been considered within mainstream architecture.

**Changing Times**

Currently, there are a growing number of architectural practices set on developing a genuine respect and understanding of Māori (and Pacific) cultures in New Zealand, including TOA Architects, Tennent Brown Architects, Monk Mackenzie, Bull O'Sullivan Architects, Jasmax and RTA Studio. This is important because traditional Māori architecture is fundamentally different from the contemporary Western approach to designing buildings, and it has a hugely significant meaning within the culture. Prior to colonisation, Māori designed their *marae* (a fenced-in complex of buildings and grounds) to incorporate a protocol and spatial sequencing for entering the *wharenui* (the meeting house); the structural elements of the *wharenui* have a direct relationship with parts of the human body, each *iwi* or tribe's ancestral links, and the place; and each building also has its own *wairua*, or spirit, identity.

Bull O'Sullivan Architecture,
Lesieli Tonga Auditorium,
Māngere, Auckland,
2017

This light and lofty auditorium, designed by Bull O'Sullivan Architecture for the Māngere branch of the Free Wesleyan Church of Tonga in Auckland, was lovingly funded and built by New Zealand's Tongan community.

Tennent Brown Architects
with Ngāi Tūhoe,
Te Wharehou o Waikaremoana,
Lake Waikaremoana,
Te Urewera,
New Zealand,
2017

Tennent Brown's new visitors' centre sits beside Lake Waikaremoana and within the beautiful Te Urewera forest. It is a controversial yet hugely important building for the Tūhoi *iwi*, who in the 1860s had been starved from their ancestral lands beside the lake by Crown forces. Today, the new centre welcomes visitors from around the world, gives Tūhoi back its identity and *mana* (status), and provides 'a conversation place' for current and future generations.

In 2005, a framework was set up for those working within the built environment to positively engage with local *iwi* groups. This was adopted by Auckland Council with the support of Ngā Aho, the society of Māori design professionals, and fed into the *Auckland Design Manual*, which states: 'Māori culture and identity highlights New Zealand's point of difference in the world and offers up significant design opportunities that can benefit us all.' Its implicit aim is to 'shape our built environment to acknowledge our position as a city in the South Pacific'.[2]

Somewhat unusual within architecture, the framework focuses on 'core values' in the form of holistic hospitality, respect for people and culture, a spiritual connection between people and land, managing and conserving the environment, unity, cohesion and collaboration. Since 2016, New Zealand has also hosted two international indigenous design conferences, and in 2017 a values-based covenant (*kawenata*) formalised an ongoing relationship between Ngā Aho and the New Zealand Institute of Architects.

## Bicultural Collaboration

This bicultural understanding of architecture, adopted from both designer and client perspectives, enables a collaborative relationship to form through the process of building, and creates an outcome that celebrates both parties, suggests Monk Mackenzie architect Raukura Turei. She is currently leading a large retail headquarters project at Auckland Airport, on an important Māori site at Waiohua, and believes we are only at the beginning of a conversation to define the identity of a New Zealand architecture.

The Māori worldview (Te Ao Māori) offers a wealth of knowledge, a connection to place and a deep respect for both the physical and natural environments. While it is not necessarily the right approach to adopt for all building projects in New Zealand, Turei believes it is the point of difference that can set its contemporary built landscape apart from the rest of the world. 'The conversation begins with empathy and the ability to listen so that genuine engagement with Tangata Whenua [Māori people of the land] and Māori practitioners in the industry can happen.'[3]

This perspective is a different concept for Western architects, but through gaining a greater understanding of Māori values, New Zealand's architecture is gaining its own unique identity and what Māori would describe as '*mana*', or status. ∆

### Notes
1. Julia Gatley (ed), *Group Architects: Towards a New Zealand Architecture*, Auckland University Press (Auckland), 2010, p 22.
2. Auckland Council, *Auckland Design Manual*: www.aucklanddesignmanual.co.nz/design-subjects/maori-design/te_aranga_principles.
3. Interview with the author, 22 January 2019.

RTA Studio, Tūrama House, Rotorua, New Zealand, 2018

A new typology, Tūrama is a house filled with stories containing an intricate layering of a family's history and the place in which it is sited. The retreat was conceived not only for its owner Professor Paul Tapsell and his immediate *whānau* (family), but for his extended Te Arawa *hapu* (sub-tribe), both current and future generations.

TOA Architects, Māori modular housing, 2019

The high cost of land, a shortage of skilled labour, and the lack of quality design are major problems affecting housing in New Zealand. TOA's modular housing design tackles these issues with a plan to build 1,000 modular houses by the end of 2020 by speeding up the build process using off-site panellised construction and cross-laminated timber technology.

FIGURE
FIGURE
FIGURE

LEADERSHIP AND SUCCESSION

FIGURE

FIGURE

FIGURE

# HEADS
Caroline Cole

# HEADS

# HEADS

## IN ARCHITECTURAL PRACTICE

# HEADS

# HEADS

These two Grade II-listed buildings are designed by very different hands, but both are credited to Arup Associates, one of the few practices in the 1970s to eschew naming its architects.

Colander Associates are experts in offering support and advice for architectural business development. The London firm's director **Caroline Cole** here explores various aspects of figurehead branding, with its 'lone genius' myth, as well as more collaborative modes of practice and their consequent corporate identity.

What is an architect? A creative maestro afforded genius status, or a lowly member of the 'supply chain', simply following orders?

In today's eclectic world, the answer is both – oh, and everything in between. So, it is unsurprising that there is no right or wrong way to lead an architectural practice. Some highly successful firms have strong figureheads, some a balanced leadership team and, increasingly, others have no figureheads at all.

Architects are taught – and tradition therefore has it – that the individual is paramount. Indeed, the archetypal architect's practice always had a maestro's name over the door. Predictably, tradition also had it that most practices did not survive their founders. History is littered with amazing practices that quietly died when the founders retired: think about Powell and Moya, Denys Lasdun & Partners or even R. Seifert and Partners, all of which have disappeared.

Ayre Chamberlain Gaunt,
206-unit build-to-rent
housing scheme,
Cardiff,
due for completion 2021

*below:* This collaboration for PLATFORM_, between Ayre Chamberlain Gaunt and a well-known Dutch precast concrete manufacturer that specialises in the design, fabrication and installation of offsite panellised buildings, illustrates how a new generation of architects is embracing design integration with manufacturing.

JTP Studios,
Bow River Village, London,
2009–

Aplb,
Advanced Technology Centre,
Eastleigh College, Eastleigh,
Hampshire,
2017

*both right:* Bow River Village for Southern Housing Group, which won the Best Large Development in the National Housing Awards 2019, and the Advanced Technology Centre, which won the Education Estates Award for Innovation in Delivering Value in 2018, are fine examples of how clients in the public sector gravitate to second- and third-generation specialist practices with collaborative leadership structures.

## Collaborative Working

The idea of doing away with the figurehead is a relatively new, 20th-century invention pioneered in the UK by Arup Associates and BDP, and in more recent history picked up by firms like muf, FAT, Architecture 00 and Assemble, all of which also come from interdisciplinary roots. For practices like these, the non-figurehead-naming strategy may have been driven by a collaborative approach to the built environment, but for others it has become a logical conclusion to changes in the way architects are perceived. There is now a myriad of specialists tramping over the architect's traditional role, making it hard for one person to stand out as the author of a project and, just as critically, pragmatic, risk-averse clients are turning to project managers and contractors to provide project leadership.

Both of these factors are unlikely to go away any time soon, especially given the now well-established procurement routes that place anyone but the architect at the head of many projects. Equally, looking to the future and the rise of modern methods of construction, many architects, like Ayre Chamberlain Gaunt, are designing directly and collaboratively with manufacturers, further blurring the edges of design ownership.

In a world that is moving rapidly towards collaborative input, it is beginning to feel as though an architectural practice that is focused on a single genius is rather old fashioned and increasingly unsustainable. So, how does the modern world perceive these organisations?

## Risk Aversion

There is no doubt that many clients, particularly those working in the public sector and large corporations, are terrified of the prospect of working with a 'maestro'. These clients – and their often risk-averse organisations – find reassurance in practices that present with a multi-headed leadership and that are, seemingly therefore, less reliant on an individual's ego. For these clients, the relationship with their architects is purely business; indeed, many will subcontract the relationship to others to manage.

Today, this client base is growing and, in response, innumerable multi-headed practices have emerged, often with three-letter acronym names that signal their transition to second- or third-generation leadership. They promote themselves as sector experts, and all studiously avoid an ego-led naming strategy: JTP, PRP and PTE in housing; Aplb, ADP and MJP in education; SOM, PLP and KPF in the commercial sector. Unless you know them well, in most of these firms you would be hard pressed to name the individual leaders of the business.

Grimshaw has turned its founder's name into a brand under which the new cohort of directors continues to deliver projects in the Nicholas Grimshaw and Partners idiom. London Bridge Station, for Thameslink, is the latest in a line of transport projects, with an impressive list of awards, including winner of the World Architecture Festival Transport – Completed Buildings category and the British Transport Awards Station of the Year, both in 2018. In 2019 it was shortlisted for the RIBA Stirling Prize.

## Client as Patron

Interestingly though, at the other end of the client spectrum, 'patron clients', with the glory projects that are so sought after by many architects, will always warm to practices that are led by figureheads. Wealthy benefactors of arts organisations, leaders of family businesses, politicians looking to raise their own profiles and those of their cities: by their very nature, these clients are able to make their own decisions without reference to audit committees or even end users. They will have a brand to promote and a legacy to establish, and they will select their architect to align with their own image.

Perhaps the most iconic example of this approach is the Guggenheim Museum in Bilbao (1997) by Frank Gehry, which is credited with single-handedly catapulting the city onto the cultural map so that now, other aspirational conurbations are lining up to use architecture to re-create the 'Bilbao Effect'. It is hard to imagine these clients engaging the services of a practice with a three-letter acronym.

## Successful Succession

Unsurprisingly, succession is hugely challenging for maestro-led practices. Their clients relish the prestige of the personal relationship and will be suspicious of a new leadership, especially one that is populated with those who have previously taken a supporting role.

But just as challenging are the changing dynamics required within the practice. The maestro himself (and it usually is a he) needs to 'let go'. This can be tough, partly because obvious successors rarely exist within these practices. Young, aspiring architects are more than happy to fly under the banner of a famous name because they get to work on amazing projects, but as time goes by the desire for personal recognition comes to the fore. As a result, the most talented individuals, who also possess leadership qualities, tend to fly the coop. Those that remain and support the maestro may well be talented, but many find it hard to step into a great leader's shoes, especially if they have thrived in supporting roles.

In all honesty, the simple replacement of a figurehead is nigh on impossible

Rogers Stirk Harbour +
Partners, Leadenhall Building,
City of London,
2014

Richard Rogers Partnership, now Rogers Stirk
Harbour + Partners, is a rare example of a
practice attempting to install a new generation
of figureheads. The Leadenhall Building for
The British Land Company Plc and Oxford
Properties, which is very obviously from the
RRP stable, is credited to Senior Design Partner
Graham Stirk, and maintains the practice's
award-winning ways, receiving the BCO Award
for Best Commercial Workplace in the UK in
2016 and a RIBA National Award in 2018.

Architects can no longer
deliver everything on
their own and that
needs, somehow, to
be reflected in the
way they present
themselves to the world

In all honesty, the simple replacement of a figurehead is nigh on impossible, and successful succession often requires the pain of jumping a generation, or a change to the unfamiliar territory of becoming a brand without a figurehead.

Some practices hope to retain some of the stardust of the maestro by turning his name into a brand: think of Nicholas Grimshaw and Partners, which is now Grimshaw, or Terry Farrell & Partners, now Farrells. Others join the ranks of the ubiquitous three-letter acronym firms: these days, not many people remember that HOK was originally Hellmuth, Obata + Kassabaum, or that EPR was Elsom Pack Roberts. A few, very few, try to install new figureheads. The most high-profile practice to attempt this feat is Richard Rogers Partnership, now called Rogers Stirk Harbour + Partners; having put Stirk's and Harbour's names up in lights, the practice plans to remove Richard's name within two years of his retirement.

By contrast, architectural practices that do not trade on an individual's personality find that longevity through succession planning is relatively simple, provided it is addressed in good time. Their clients are less skittish when it comes to leadership changes, and the architects working in these firms tend to understand that ego is not necessarily an asset. As a result, setting aside internal power struggles, the transition from generation to generation can be, and is, achieved with relative ease: many of the three-letter acronym brigade are now onto their third or fourth generations.

There is no doubt that a practice that is built in the image of several individuals with complementary skills will appeal to a wide range of clients with conventional projects, but it is also true that the romance of employing a maestro will, inevitably, appeal to many with the most coveted projects. It is therefore reassuring that as one of the few contributors to our built environment that straddles art and science, craft and technology, whimsy and pragmatism, architects are able to respond with variety and diversity. But we must not forget: whether they are autocratic or collaborative, architects can no longer deliver everything on their own and that needs, somehow, to be reflected in the way they present themselves to the world. Đ

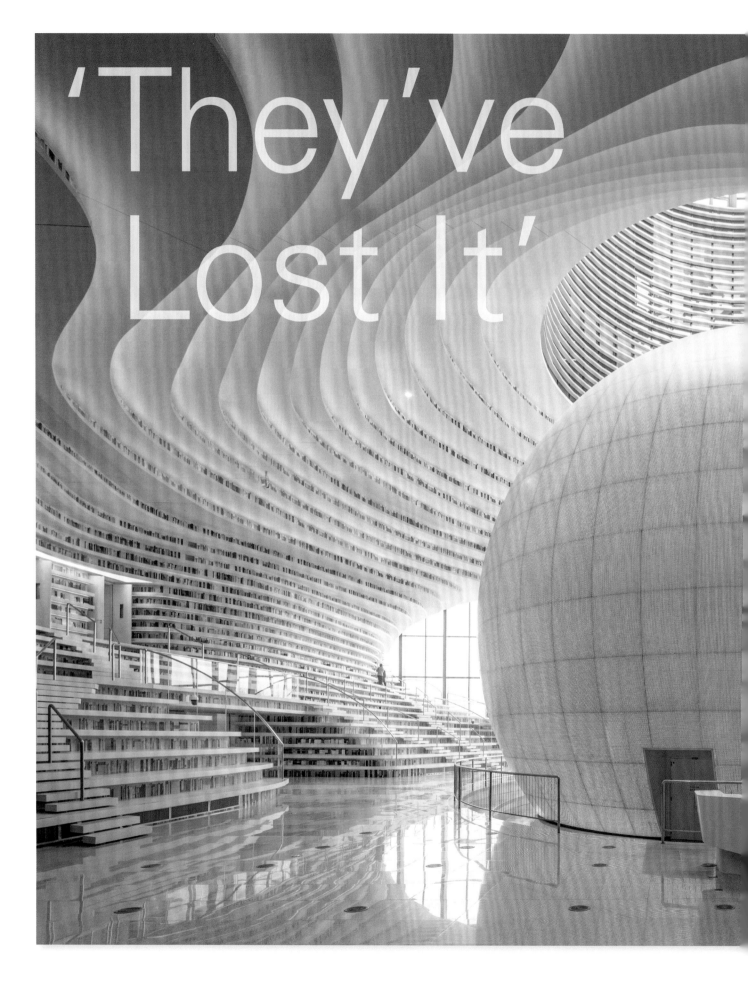

'They've Lost It'

# A Balancing Act: MVRDV and the Language of Marketing

**Jan Knikker**

MVRDV,
Tianjin Binhai Library,
Tianjin,
China,
2017

The five-level building, with a luminous spherical auditorium and floor-to-ceiling cascading bookcases, contains diverse educational facilities arrayed along the edges of the interior and accessed through the main atrium, and also functions as a social space and connector to the cultural district.

**Jan Knikker** spent a decade honing the public and professional image of OMA before joining MVRDV, another Rotterdam-based international practice, in 2008 and running its business development, contracts and public relations. He describes MVRDV's corporate communications with clients, which are built on a foundation of speaking their language and being pragmatic. The downside is that not communicating in the sophist ways of the profession can alienate architects from themselves.

MVRDV,
Valley,
Amsterdam,
The Netherlands,
2015

A multifunctional building in the Zuidas Business District of Amsterdam, Valley includes a mixed programme of offices, residences and amenities. The project derives its name from the publicly accessible terraced and green valley between its three mixed-use towers.

MVRDV,
Markthal,
Rotterdam,
The Netherlands,
2014

The Markthal was formed by the construction of privately developed apartments arranged into a large arch, strategically allowing a private initiative to create a public space. It is a sustainable combination of food, leisure, living and parking, a building in which all functions are fully integrated, and a new landmark for the city.

If MVRDV's communication people were to use the words branding, marketing and sales, their architect colleagues would spontaneously develop a rash. The very notion of something commercial is by many architects considered bad taste – despite the fact that they, like almost all humans in the globalised world, are totally susceptible to marketing themselves, consequently selecting brands such as Camper, Comme des Garçons, Nike and Cos.

As architects try to maintain a non-commercial environment in their lives, the clients they work for on offices, retail and housing are often the total opposite. Let us exaggerate a bit: in architecture, the soul of the artist meets the hardcore capitalist interested in profit per square metre. It is no wonder that these two groups speak different languages; architects often talk about philosophical ideas for the city and their designs, while the commercial client is often more practical, discussing the project based on financial and political motives.

In architecture, the soul of the artist meets the hardcore capitalist interested in profit per square metre

## Marketing and PR

It is for this reason that MVRDV started a business development (BD) team. Being at the time an office of 60 people, the practice was able to afford staff with a background in business who can talk to developers in their own language and translate the architects' ideals about architecture and urbanism into fee proposals and contracts. Business development (or marketing) means direct contact with clients and potential clients; there is also a public relations effort that precedes it. First, the PR team works on the reputation of the practice with an open-ended, long-term public relations strategy that involves talking to a broad section of society to explain the work; then follow the BD people, making deals with clients who hopefully, by then, already know MVRDV.

In this communication effort, the language used is key. Architects' use of the word 'volume', a standard term in the profession, can already be quite challenging for some people and is an example of highly sophisticated yet often inaccessible 'archispeak'. The firm's PR and BD teams try to keep the language on the level of a general newspaper in order to be accessible. Knowing that only a small number of the practice's clients have studied architecture, it is simply a matter of politeness to speak in a way that those being addressed can understand. This fits perfectly into MVRDV's democratic philosophy to bring great architecture to a wide range of people. It is an approach to communication that relates to its architecture, as the practice is always looking for the best possible solution to a client or user's question. As architecture in MVRDV's view is an applied art, there is a strong sense of practicality in its philosophy.

MVRDV,
Casa Kwantes,
Rotterdam,
The Netherlands,
2016

A contemporary take on 1930s Modernism, the wall of brickwork on the street side of the house responds to the clients' desire for seclusion and privacy, while fluid glass walls sweeping around the living spaces on the garden side simultaneously offer maximum daylight and open living spaces. Sustainable solutions including a ground-source heat pump, heat exchange system and solar panels on the roof ensure a limited environmental footprint.

For an architecture office such as MVRDV, PR and BD offer a sense of great authenticity and integrity because the work has an idealistic foundation

MVRDV,
Floriade 2022,
Almere,
The Netherlands,
2022

Floriade 2022 is the world's largest horticultural expo. MVRDV imagines the area in Almere as a green extension to the city centre, a lasting *cité idéale*. The ambition is to increase Almere's size while simultaneously improving the quality of life for its inhabitants, including transforming the lake into a central feature of the city to connect its disparate neighbourhoods.

## Public Ideal

This is simply a matter of translation and not a different way of working. MVRDV is often asked if marketing drives its designs and whether it creates 'Instagram architecture'. The answer is no: the design teams are independent and work within their ideals according to the client's brief. PR and BD are practical second steps that come after the design – enhancing the firm's reputation and enabling the architects to work on new projects in future.

For an architecture office such as MVRDV, PR and BD offer a sense of great authenticity and integrity because the work has an idealistic foundation, in that the foremost purpose of an architect is to provide shelter and take responsibility for the planet. Even though it is a healthy capitalist entity, profit is not MVRDV's only objective, and in this sense its branding and PR are certainly run with a very public ideal, which is also manifest, for example, in helping students whenever possible.

The downside of this practical approach is that MVRDV cannot impress or intimidate with intricate language that adds the layer of intellect needed to connect its projects with their abstract philosophies. It is therefore more difficult for peers to fully grasp the depth of the projects; in their online comments, they shower the work with claims that MVRDV have 'lost it'– about works which, in any case, are loved by the public. So somehow, while MVRDV has solved the issue of client communication up to a point, it appears to have lost touch with its peers – which is the next great challenge to answer. ⌂

MVRDV,
Vanke 3D City,
Shenzhen,
China,
2018

The Vanke Group headquarters building provides office space for the real-estate company's staff and forms a vibrant mixed-use city block containing plentiful outdoor spaces. The stack of eight blocks that make up Vanke 3D City are designed to strike a balance between architectural diversity and cohesiveness.

Text © 2019 John Wiley & Sons Ltd. Images: pp 104-5, 107, 108-9(t) photos Ossip van Duivenbode; p 106 Image Vero Visuals; pp 108(b), 109(b) © MVRDV

Jay Merrick

Allford Hall Monaghan Morris (AHMM),
Weston Street apartments,
Bermondsey,
London,
2017

Working with developer Solidspace, AHMM's scheme
provides eight split-level apartments, with a large
office space on the ground floor. The apartments' open-
plan configurations of living, kitchen and study spaces
across three levels produce a strongly sculptural play
of interlocking units.

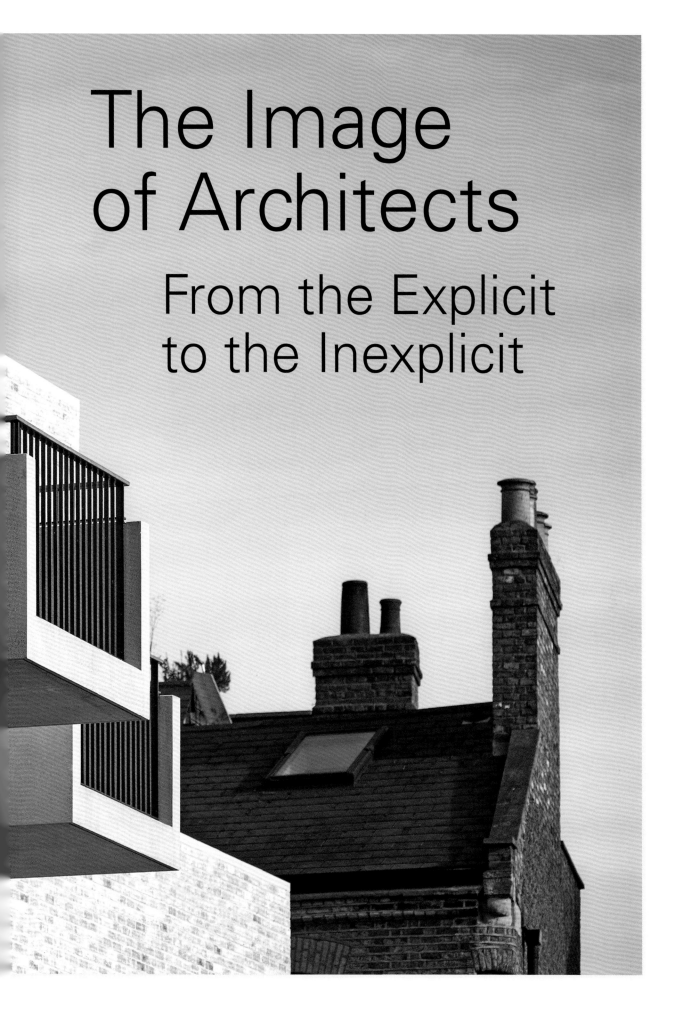

# The Image
# of Architects

## From the Explicit
## to the Inexplicit

Does size matter?
Is it possible to retain the flavour and ambition of the work of an up-and-coming practice after it becomes successful, or large and international? Based in London, architectural journalist and critic **Jay Merrick** discusses and illustrates this conundrum, looking at a few practices and how their design prima materia is continually open to question.

Skidmore, Owings & Merrill (SOM), Assemble, Kengo Kuma. What do these randomly chosen names signify? What essential image or ethos do they convey? Are their images solid ingots of presence and architectural intention, or more like superficial brandmarks? The images of architects or practices may suggest the cerebral, the commercial, the civic or even the venal, but do they communicate any sense of deeper commitment to the way buildings, places and lives progress?

In JG Ballard's 1973 novel *Crash*, the narrator says: 'After being bombarded endlessly by road-safety propaganda it was almost a relief to find myself in an actual accident.'[1] In an age now dominated by a restless and relentless churn of information, imagery and production, the images of most architects and practices have become subspecies of propaganda. How often are we relieved to encounter, beyond the propaganda, the actual and meaningful image of a practice?

It is, though, often difficult to assign a genuinely engaging image to particular architects or practices, while associations with particular architectural genres are not always helpful in terms of defining their image. Overused generic labels – Modernist, Postmodernist, High Tech – have the scent of embalming fluid.

Allford Hall Monaghan Morris (AHMM),
AEP Fitness Center/Oklahoma City Ballet,
Oklahoma,
2015

The AEP Fitness Center extends an unused basement structure in northern Oklahoma City into a sports and leisure hub. A series of arched steel trusses, clad internally with sheet metal, were placed over the existing concrete basement to enclose the hangar-like volume.

The passing of time may well help to resolve the image of particular architects. We have an immediate sense of the beliefs and form-making characteristics and qualities of, for example, Nicholas Hawksmoor, Joseph Paxton, Konstantin Melnikov, Frank Lloyd Wright, Oscar Niemeyer or Kenzo Tange. Le Corbusier was the first 20th-century architect to radiate a persistent, polemically projected image both in terms of his work, beginning with his Plan Voisin and Esprit Nouveau Pavilion in Paris (1925) and his personal aura, his appearance framed by those emphatically 'visionary' Maison Bonnet spectacle frames.

Similarly, it is reasonable to suggest that by 2000 the image of Zaha Hadid Architects was a compaction of four visions: the 1993 Vitra Fire Station at Weil am Rhein, Germany; Hadid's Garboesque presence; her brilliant post-Suprematist drawings; and densely argued theoretical rationales. Patrik Schumacher spoke then of 'the new ontology defining what it means to be somewhere'.[2] ZHA now offers new 'somewheres' attractive to very different clients worldwide.

**The Curse of Bigness**
However, as successful architects buoyed by strong identities have found themselves increasingly in demand in an expanding global economy, the question arises as to how they can sustain and nurture the very identity that made them so attractive and allowed them to grow in the first place.

The 'curse of bigness',[3] a phrase coined in 1913 by Louis Brandeis, the legendary anti-cartel American Supreme Court judge, challenges both the image of a profuse practice and its contribution to the art or public value of architecture. When we think of SOM, for example, do we associate their ethos and image with the Burj Khalifa (2010) in Dubai – sheer bigness, however masterfully achieved – or with historically innovative buildings such as the US Air Force Academy Cadet Chapel in Colorado Springs or Yale's Beinecke Library at New Haven, both completed in 1963?

An increasing bigness in architectural proclamations has become synonymous with the global growth of fecund international practices, and the sheer volume of press releases they produce evokes *grande bouffe* qualities and shock-and-awe architectural production. Can all their schemes be so truly remarkable, so thought-provoking, and of such significant cultural or technical importance that we must be told about them so unremittingly?

The image of a practice is, in fact, far clearer and more resonant if, regardless of its architectural approach or scale of production, it imparts a belief in architecture as a culturally engaged force. Ironically, though, even the most

Skidmore, Owings & Merrill (SOM),
US Air Force Academy Cadet Chapel,
Colorado Springs,
Colorado,
1963

The Cadet Chapel was the final element of SOM's masterplan and individual building designs for the US Air Force Academy campus. The chapel features 17 glass and aluminium spires, each composed of 100 tetrahedrons. The building has Protestant, Catholic and Jewish chapels.

Skidmore, Owings & Merrill (SOM),
Burj Khalifa,
Dubai,
2010

This 828-metre (2,716-foot) high mixed-use tower, with 162 storeys, was designed under the leadership of SOM design partner Adrian Smith. The architecture, supported by innovative structural and environmental technology, was inspired by the geometries of a desert flower, and by classic Islamic patterns.

dynamic motivations can be obscured if an architect's image is too distinct. For example, to think of Richard Neutra is to tripwire a default collage of his gleaming Case Study houses (1945–8). But how many of us would simultaneously remember that these houses were commissioned by *Arts & Architecture* magazine,[4] and reflected the profound environmental concerns that Neutra later explained in his book, *Survival Through Design* (1953).[5]

In general, though, there is the sense of a gradual reduction of architectural beliefs as the centrally communicated ingredient of practices' images. Practices tend to lose their original images, and histories, in the slipstream of architectural consumerism. Recently some of Britain's established practices have reacted to this. Allford Hall Monaghan Morris (AHMM), for example, a big and prolific practice, have striven to reignite their germinal image based on the design of novel early buildings like Great Notley Primary School, and the Peabody flats in Dalston, London (both 1999). Their Weston Street apartments (2017) and buildings in Oklahoma City completed in 2014 have an interesting *à la recherche de l'aventure perdue* quality, which modulates the practice's commercial image.

Branding can affect the way such practices are perceived. Towards the end of 2018, Duggan Morris Architects, perhaps the most rapidly successful of Britain's younger

practices, was renamed Morris+Company; the new name suggests a reductive let's-do-business vibe even as the practice branches out into some new and less commercial architectural territories.

In the case of Architype, their image as environmentally led architects is crystal clear in their portfolio, and in the design of their website and business cards. Thinking of Peter Barber instantly triggers visions of brilliantly original low-cost housing.

Some practices' images are distilled from subtly layered ideas about architectural meaning. Consider 6a architects, whose design approach expresses qualities such as bricolage, inexactness, witty deceptions and palimpsests. This has produced several conceptually (and actually) interesting buildings, the latest being the transformed and extended MK Gallery in Milton Keynes. The practice has a non-polemical reputation based on what the eminent academic Irénée Scalbert summarises with a single word – 'curiosity'.[6]

The image of another notable small practice, Lynch Architects, is embedded in a profound concern with architecture's civic agency, and the way history and intuition can produce designs expressing the phenomena of time and place. It could be said that the practice's image is composed of the bricks of their architecture, and the mortar of various books, critical writings and their bi-annual *Journal of Civic Architecture*.

Lynch Architects,
*Mimesis*,
2015

*Mimesis* explores the work of Lynch Architects, focusing on the practice's interest in architectural mimesis and civic architecture, and their recent major buildings in Victoria Street, London. The book, published by Artifice, also highlights their collaborative practice with artists and designers including Rut Blees Luxemburg and Timorous Beasties.

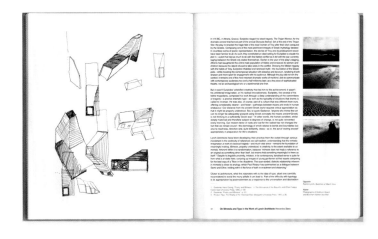

Patrick Lynch,
*Civic Ground*,
2018

Patrick Lynch traces the philosophical background to the work of his practice in a book that originated as a PhD thesis supervised by Peter Carl, Helen Mallinson and Joseph Rykwert. *Civic Ground* questions the comparison of architecture with sculpture, arguing that parallels should also be seen in terms of rhythmic spatiality.

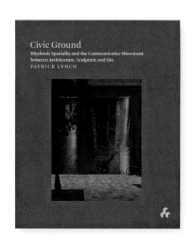

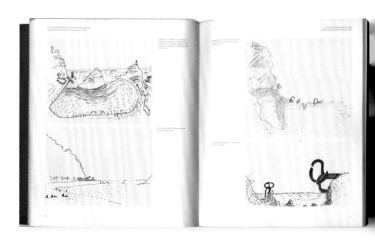

Lynch Architects,
*Journal of Civic Architecture,*
2018

This biannual journal edited by Patrick Lynch gathers essays, visual essays, poetry, drawings and architecture that relate to photography, literature and city life. The subjects range from the academic to the quizzical. Contributors have included Johan Celsing, John Meunier, Joseph Rykwert, Tom de Paor, Cino Zucchi and Laura Evans.

Ultimately, of course, any discussion of practices and their images can only be quixotic. Architectural anarchists or loners, such as Lebbeus Woods and Peter Zumthor, project images or presences that are dynamically strange because they are simultaneously resonant and fugitive. As JG Ballard suggested so presciently in 1974, we exist in a sea of fictions in which merchandising and politics operate as advertising. He likened it to existing inside an enormous novel: 'The fiction is already there. The writer's task is to invent the reality.'[7] The architect's increasingly difficult task is to build, and communicate, reality as if it were a truth rather than a fiction. ᴆ

### Notes

1. JG Ballard, *Crash*, Fourth Estate (London), 2014, p 28.
2. Patrik Schumacher, 'In Defence of Radicalism: On the Work of Zaha Hadid', *City Visionaries* catalogue for the British Pavilion, Venice Architecture Biennale, Cornerhouse Publications (Manchester), 2000, p 13.
3. Louis Brandeis, 'A Curse of Bigness', *Harper's Weekly*, 10 January 1913, p 18.
4. John Entenza, 'The Case Study House Program', *Arts & Architecture*, January 1945, pp 37–9.
5. Richard Neutra, *Survival Through Design*, Oxford University Press (New York), 1953.
6. Irénée Scalbert and 6a architects, *Never Modern*, Park Books (Zurich), 2013, p 20.
7. Zadie Smith, 'Introduction' in JG Ballard, *op cit*, p vii.

6a architects,
Juergen Teller Studio,
North Kensington,
London,
2016

This studio and home for photographer Juergen Teller is in a three-building enfilade on a long, narrow site, punctuated by gardens designed by Dan Pearson Studio. The materiality and qualities of light are inspired by RSR Fitter's book *London's Natural History* (1945) and by the architecture of Sir John Soane.

# HOLDING ON TO OUR PRINCIPLES

Thomas Bryans

## WHY MANIFESTOES MATTER

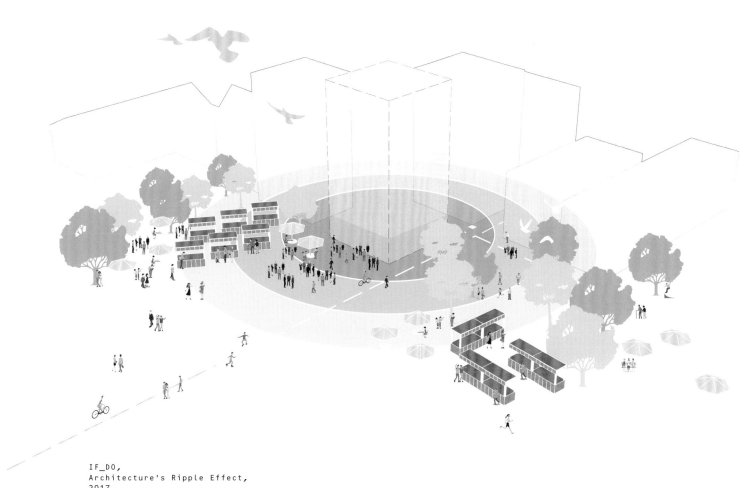

IF_DO,
Architecture's Ripple Effect,
2017

What if all buildings were designed to produce positive ripple effects,
improving the communities around them by consciously optimising their
social, environmental and economic impact in creating a better future for all?

Forming a fledgling architectural practice can be challenging and the ideals of its founders buffeted in the wake of commercial realism. **Thomas Bryans** describes his UK studio, IF_DO, and their establishment of a manifesto of preoccupations and objectives to keep them on target.

With no work, no clients, and – at the point that it was written – no prospective leads, why the need to write a manifesto? As Bernard Tschumi has written, '"manifestoes" resemble contracts that the undersigned make with themselves and with society'.[1] For IF_DO, as a new practice, it was an intentionally optimistic declaration of intent, a commitment to the world, and a marker against which the studio could be judged both by itself and by others.

Its co-founders graduated in the immediate aftermath of the 2008 recession, which was followed a year later by the widely perceived failure of the UN Climate Change Conference in Copenhagen, and in 2011 by the London Riots, caused, in part, by increasing inequality. Three crises – financial, environmental and social – have continued, on a global scale, to define the decade or so since.

IF_DO,
Joseph Walsh Studio,
County Cork,
Ireland,
2016

*right:* Located in rural Ireland, this furniture studio and workshop was designed to create a profound connection to place for its users, through its architecture, but also by ensuring contact with nature and outdoor spaces.

IF_DO,
St Teresa's Sixth Form Centre,
Effingham,
Surrey,
2018

*left:* Extensive research has demonstrated the benefit of views of trees and greenery to student wellbeing and educational outcomes. This was central to the design of the St Teresa's Sixth Form Centre, which improves connections to the green spaces around the building and brings nature into its centre.

## CREATING OUR CULTURES

Architecture, of course, did not cause these crises, but nor is it innocent. Architecture is a reflection of the time in which it is created, and of the values of the society that produces it. As Peter Buchanan has argued, one of the fundamental purposes of architecture 'is as a means for creating our cultures and ourselves'.[2]

This was the context in which discussions about the vague outline of a practice began in early 2014. The starting point was not an aesthetic vision or a defined sector in which to operate, but rather a set of fundamental principles around which to work to create architecture that benefits all members of a community by harnessing construction's economic, environmental and social ripples for positive effect.

It is easy, however, to make such a statement before producing any work. It is far harder to stick to in the messy reality of architectural practice. Such is that challenge, that Tschumi also described manifestoes as being 'like love letters', in that 'they provide an erotic distance between fantasy and actual realisation'.[3]

# Architecture is a reflection of the time in which it is created, and of the values of the society that produces it

IF_DO,
Little Horsecroft Cottage,
Bury St Edmunds,
Suffolk,
2018

This 18th-century farmhouse was saved from dereliction by an environmentally led restoration and extension that has resulted in a reduction in $CO_2$ emissions from heating of 78 per cent, with all energy and water generated and sourced on site.

# To design public places where all the people feel welcome the practice believes that the design team needs to be as diverse as the community it is designing for

IF_DO,
Albion Street,
Rotherhithe,
London,
2020

A 10-year meanwhile project, this building will provide low-cost office space to local start-ups and small businesses. A contentious site, the design process involved extensive work with the surrounding community to ensure that it was serving their needs.

IF_DO,
Granby Place,
London, 2017

Supported by the Mayor's Air Quality Fund as part of a wider project for a new community hub, Granby Place transformed an existing backyard into a new public square, and also extended the adjacent Lower Marsh market.

## FOUNDING PRINCIPLES

In the five years that IF_DO has been operating, its manifesto – effectively a series of questions and ambitions[4] – has acted as both a reference point and a marker for where the practice aims to go. It challenges the team, as was the intention, not to lose sight of the practice's founding principles.

At its heart are four central themes: wellbeing, the environment, inclusivity and connection to place. These ideas, along with the broader beliefs that underpin them, have and continue to shape both the culture of how the studio practices, as well as the work it produces.

To take inclusivity as but one example, to design public places where all people feel welcome the practice believes that the design team needs to be as diverse as the community it is designing for. It is a principle that should apply to all projects, but particularly so to meanwhile ones (temporary usage prior to more permanent development), which often signify the changing character of an area. The realisation of IF_DO's meanwhile projects – Granby Space and Place (2017) and Albion Street (due for completion 2020), both in London – has involved extensive input from local volunteers, which creates a sense of community pride and ownership.

Of course, not every project can fulfil all of the practice's aspirations. IF_DO's manifesto is therefore more about a direction of travel than a series of absolutes for how the studio must operate. It helps to set a course, but like sailing into the wind it will take tacking from side to side to get there. △

Notes
1. Bernard Tschumi, *Architectural Manifestoes*, Architectural Association (London), 1979, p 1.
2. Peter Buchanan, 'The Big Rethink Part 4: The Purpose of Architecture', *Architectural Review*, 1382, April 2012, p 78.
3. Tschumi, *op cit*, p 1.
4. See www.ifdo.co/practice#manifesto.

IF_DO,
Dulwich Pavilion,
Dulwich Picture Gallery,
London,
2017

Commissioned to celebrate the Dulwich Picture Gallery's bicentenary, the pavilion was instrumental in increasing the diversity of audience to the gallery. It is to be relocated to a local primary school to become a covered outdoor play area, ensuring a lasting benefit for the local community.

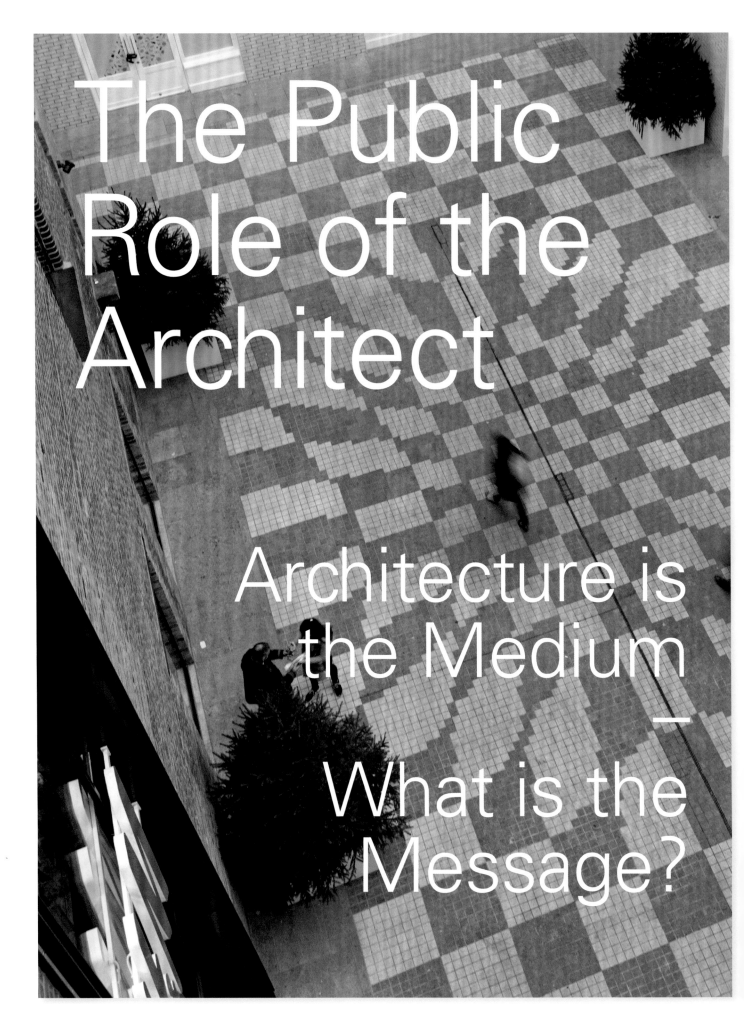

# The Public Role of the Architect

## Architecture is the Medium
—
## What is the Message?

At a time of worldwide political fractionalisation and growing social and economic disparity, **Ian Ritchie** discusses the public role, responsibilities and self-created myths of the architect and how these are conveyed vis-à-vis society, the public, the profession and the wider world.

Ian Ritchie Architects,
Mercer Walk,
Covent Garden,
London,
2016

The Mercer Walk concept creates part of a new east–west pedestrian route through Covent Garden. At its heart is a new piazza reflecting and reinforcing the *genius loci* and urban structure of this part of the city. Orientation is made simple through the massing of traditional warehouse forms, each with its own colour, and through the paving design.

Communication is the very essence of architecture: a building's materials and fabric, form, and relationship with its environment convey encoded messages to the public and users interacting with it. While transmitting specific information about how the building is to be used and experienced, they also record the cultural and financial ambitions of those who commissioned it, the economic and sociopolitical structures and values embodied by its brief, and the architect's aesthetic intentions.

Although individual architects must be able to communicate effectively to complete a project, as a collective architects seem unable to revive the profession's dwindling reputation with the general public and its reduced intellectual role in contemporary public life. Our social- and digital-media-saturated age suggests the solution of hiring marketing and brand-identity firms to reposition architecture's image, but before doing so we should ask ourselves whether we have in fact sought the public's approval during the last few decades.

Unlike other media, architecture exists within and changes the real space it inhabits. The consequences of its messages are real and long-lasting because architecture transforms the economic and political ideologies it embodies into the world in which people live and interact. Buildings and spaces shape and structure, facilitate and limit the human emotions, interactions and activities that take place within them: architecture has an inescapable civic and political content.

It follows that we have an ethical obligation to the public, as well as to the client and our own art, to create spaces in which human flourishing and social progress can best occur, and which support the state of physical, mental and social wellbeing which the World Health Organization defines as 'health'.[1]

Too many architects have abdicated these professional and ethical responsibilities. Responding to financialised housing markets that cater to the preferences of wealthy global investors and individuals rather than the needs of communities, a media-fuelled orgy of architectural narcissism has resulted in stylistically incoherent cityscapes dominated by buildings lacking any sensitivity to each other, cultural context or community aesthetic traditions, expressive of little more than the desire to be iconic.

Architects who regard themselves as experts in creating environments for users who are not conscious of formal design principles, and whose aesthetic values may differ from theirs, have ignored the public's valid and justifiably strong opinions about the places in which they live and work. Worst of all, the unashamed commerciality of the profession has created cities and developments explicitly supporting the notion of inequality. They present glittering facades to people who cannot afford to live there, exacerbating divides along economic and social fault lines and fuelling political discontent.

The architectural profession has actually been conveying a clear message to a public who have no real choice about the degree to which they interact with the environments we create and little say in the design process: they do not matter. Why should a public whose opinions and needs we do not care about respect us? It is no surprise if public opinion discounts the profession's benefits and exaggerates its flaws.

Ian Ritchie Architects,
Farsons Old Brewhouse and
Trident Business Park,
Mriehel,
Malta,
2017

At Trident Business Park, wayfinding is communicated and facilitated primarily by the use of colour. Straight covered external routes – at each floor level and connecting all buildings – offer views into the gardens either side of each building.

# The unashamed commerciality of the profession has created cities and developments explicitly supporting the notion of inequality

The gardens and vertical circulation towers located at the south end of each garden at Trident Business Park are colour themed. Vertical circulation between the buildings is shared by everyone and is designed to encourage interaction and use of the gardens, which are a traditional spatial structure of the old Maltese palaces.

The centre's west end provides a small public park, and at night images are projected on to the building's white cast-glass facade. The image shows a highly magnified neuron firing. The idea of a building communicating its interior activities – science research in this case – rather than commercial advertising is not new, but is an important aspect of a facade's role.

Ian Ritchie Architects,
Sainsbury Wellcome Centre for
Neural Circuits and Behaviour,
University College London (UCL),
London,
2016

The traditional colonnade communicates with passers-by through a set of five informative vitrines and a 'ceiling' of suspended pixels. The score of Bach's great Prussian fugue is printed on one side. On the other are 11 partial portraits of Nobel Laureates who have spent parts of their careers at UCL. As each viewer walks along the colonnade, their brain deals with the gaps in the retinal images by constructing complete portraits from the pixellated ones using a neural process called 'filling in'.

Throughout the building, the interior surfaces of the white, structural, insulated cast-glass facade assembly, and even the transparent openable windows it supports, are designed to be used as a handy whiteboard by scientists making notes or expressing complex ideas and calculations during discussions.

*opposite:* The Wellcome Centre's interior architecture facilitates communication by providing opportunities to collaborate and interact easily; transparent glass walls, for example, are used as whiteboards. Scientists explained to the architects that ideas often arise spontaneously during conversation, and that thoughts often need to be exchanged immediately and visually.

## Changing the Message

Changing the message requires listening, and listening begins with a commitment to awareness and understanding. Architecture still has enormous potential for delivering significant social and cultural value and there has been a perceptual shift in values and attitude within the profession, especially among the younger generation of architects and in parts of the world of minor interest to a Western-focused media.

Although the dominance of contractors has eroded the architect's influence, and the client's wishes and the planning system reduce the architect's agency, practices that apply intelligent rather than stylistically driven design, and a genuine concern with public process and end-user needs, to their projects, are creating buildings and spaces that combine beauty and functionality.

Their work is helped by the growing body of scientific evidence that is quantifying the biological, neurological and emotional ways in which architecture and environment affect human minds and behaviour. 'Designing with the mind in mind' from the inception of a project is easier knowing that a visual balance of simplicity and complexity rather than blank walls communicates accessibility to passers-by, that access to green spaces and light increases our physical and mental wellbeing, and that the ability to have some control over one's environment is crucial for human happiness. There is also less justification for ignoring such factors during the design process.

Architects who use their advantage as experts to engage with and enlighten ultimate users rather than force solutions on them gain access to their specific knowledge and experience. Doing so greatly increases the probability that their architecture – articulated according to the ultimate users' specific demands and preferences as well as aesthetic and commercial principles – will be the better for it.

Many architects find it easy to talk about what they are doing, but difficult to explain why they are doing it. Architectural concepts can be complicated, and communicating these ideas often becomes mired in discipline-specific terminology.

Developing skills to communicate at a level that a general audience can understand requires deliberate practice, careful attention to language, and a willingness to listen with the modesty that comes hard to a profession that regularly discounts the public's taste while forgetting that some of the world's most beautiful, visually intricate and complex buildings are also the most popular with the general population.

### Genuine Communication Begins with Integrity

A good place for architects to begin regaining their credibility is by cleaning our own house. If our institutions want to become the first port of call for developers, politicians and the public on questions of development and the environment, they must be seen as powerful agencies for change and good. They must become known as guarantors of integrity and intolerant of corruption – and individually we must cry out when we see it, and behave accordingly. As the late Cedric Price wrote: 'Withdrawal of labour is an activity insufficiently considered by the architectural profession.'[2]

Let us use our imaginations and skills at persuasion to ameliorate the worst architectural excesses of wealth and power. If a star architect's services are so valuable that they lend 'value' and attract funding to a project, then a bit of arm twisting by such individuals has the potential to be effective. A united front or collective boycott might be an even more powerful mechanism to help initiate change.

And most important: if as architects we want to be capable of engaging in a genuine conversation with the public and fellow professionals, our common agenda as humans and inhabitants of a planet stressed to breaking point must now outweigh all other considerations.

The real cost of every architectural project is born by every individual, society and the world as a whole. One action we could take for every design decision, independent of its apparent scale of impact, is to question its meaning and outcome for quality of life on a global level. The simple act of asking the question will help us begin to develop a critical sense. ∆

**Notes**
1. 'Health is a state of complete physical, mental and social well-being and not merely the absence of disease or infirmity.' World Health Organization, 1948: www.who.int/about/who-we-are/constitution.
2. Cedric Price, *Architecture Canada Newsmagazine*, 48, 15 February 1971, p 1: http://hdl.handle.net/10222/74874.

# THE SELFIE OF AN ARCHITECT

COUNTERPOINT
06/2019
No 262

In bringing his experience as an architect, teacher, founder of the avant-garde NATO group in the 1980s, and product and interior designer, **Nigel Coates** lets us have his personal take on the identity of the architect while evoking the importance of an architect's education and their ownership of ideas, as well as the power of social media – not for him polite corporate mediocrity and conformity.

Faced with this issue's kaleidoscopic deconstructing of the architect's identity, one problem crops up repeatedly: the confusion between the architect as an individual and the architect in practice. Is it realistic to think of the architect as a misunderstood genius, like an artist? Can a practice, consisting of many individuals, really convey 'Kunstwollen'? Is it any wonder, then, that architects themselves are confused?

## On the Skids

Architects crave respect from their peers and a degree of public recognition, but ultimately they need jobs to survive. They must put the right foot forward to stay in business. But what do other people, their potential clients and users, think of architects today? A commonly held opinion among the general public is that they vandalise the environment, no matter how much they claim to be acting for the collective good or gesture towards sustainability.

However careful you, the architect, are at maintaining that balance between creative individuality and social responsibility, to others you may still seem like a self-serving pariah in league with the developer, or at best mistakenly adhering to some architectural ideology. How often do we hear that 'what was there before was a lot better than that monstrosity'? In certain circumstance your mere presence can provoke insults if not death threats. At a fancy dinner party given by a leading fashion designer some years ago, Bob

Geldof, a guest at the very generous round dining table, leaned towards me accusatively. 'It's people like you that build those dreadful tower blocks. They kill people.'

Is it any wonder that architects find it hard to put their real passion across? Presumptions aside, the usual anodyne communication tone ties up nicely with boring clothes, dreary drawings and a bland building, however you communicate it.

If you are not sure whether your studio is a brand, a corporation or firm of consultants, what spews out in the name of PR inevitably gets watered down and misdirected. Most architects' websites are utterly formulaic, with 'about', 'projects', 'team' as typical catch-alls. There is rarely any driving message; identity arrives by accident, by word of mouth, by being featured in *Dezeen* or with success on Instagram. Keeping such a message alive is more likely to come from the tradition of teaching, writing and lecturing in architecture, all of which can act as a very stimulating boost to the banality of the office.

## Research a Must

There are exceptions of course, where chutzpah and determination win through for client and public alike. Zaha Hadid, herself a dedicated teacher for much of her career, often preferred lists to elaborate explanation, but there was always research behind her proposals. You learned by doing. During her marathon lectures, only the briefest of explanations for each of a bullet-feed of completed projects would be forthcoming. *Kunstwollen* there was in spades.

In one of the multiple perspectives offered in this issue of Δ, ZHA's Roger Howie (pp 74–9) goes behind the public face to reveal how important 'design' was for Zaha, especially by the time the practice was consistently working on many architectural projects around the world, each of which required large teams of people. Research would sometimes be put on the back burner. She took solace in her work as a designer of things – furniture, lamps, jewellery, shoes – with which she could continue mentoring her atelier as she had always done ever since her teaching days.

Indeed, when Zaha and I were young teachers at the Architectural Association (AA), research was everything. Your unit needed a strong identity or else it would literally be forced out of the 'market' of the unit system. Zaha was unique in evolving the atelier approach to what later became the first real brand in architecture, comparable to Dior and Prada, sustained throughout by her vision, curiosity and determination. Fashion brands often begin as ateliers with a single creative force at the helm. As they grow they need creative direction from one individual, and like Zaha, can be compromised by corporate scale. As Jay Merrick reminds us in this issue, they can fall victim to the 'curse of bigness' (pp 110–15).

Nigel Coates,
Art Silo and The Wall,
Tokyo,
1990

Working transparency and found imagery, this multimedia drawing juxtaposes the proposed building with an equally tall male body that reinforces an anthropomorphic reading. The head of the body sports an aerodynamic helmet that suggests change.

# Architects seem compelled to objectify their work. Rather than sign it as an artist might, they tend to hold it at a dispassionate distance

In school, the conflict between individual and practice has to be confronted from the beginning; let us say the pragmatic purpose of your training is that one day you will get a job, and someone will pay you for it. But architecture is a calling, a way of life; it is totally immersive and you are learning to be part of a community driven by what matters to you and to other architects. In the end it is a very individual affair. You are judged by designing an entire building on your own, a task that as a professional you are never likely to repeat. And in the modern world of architectural business, this divide has deepened.

## Take Back Control

Architects seem compelled to objectify their work. Rather than sign it as an artist might, they tend to hold it at a dispassionate distance. But it is patently absurd to pretend that who you are as a person has nothing to do with the work you produce. If you are a boring person with few ideas of your own, it follows that you will produce boring work.

Stereotyping is rife, and many battles still have to be won. Women architects are familiar with this conundrum, and risk being interpreted as weak by the architectural establishment. To push their design agendas, women architects may feel the need to resort to the forcefulness and arrogant behaviour of some men. Indeed, Zaha was often said to have balls. Equally, if a man enjoys fluid shapes and lots of fabric, and is inclined to the interior rather than the mega-project, he may also be dismissed as excelling at interiors. In many fields other than architecture, queerness has become an unstoppable liberating force. In the fashion world it is taken as a given that many of the top creatives are gay, and they won't be afraid for this oscillating identity to show on the catwalk. Not so in architecture. Minorities, whether gendered or ethnic, are the exception. The average architect is at best a metro-sexual, probably white male, dependable and stylish, but not too so.

Massimiliano and
Doriana Fuksas,
Rome,
2016

The Fuksases have a strict policy of appearing together, emphasising the joint authorship of their entire practice output, whether it be architecture or design. Their stylish portraits use black-and-white photography to reinforce their brand.

For grandee architects, a cultivated self-image works in support of the output of the office, like Bernard Tschumi's red scarf or Massimiliano and Doriana Fuksas's double black-and-white portraits. In the case of Tschumi, the scarf reinforces his use of red as an activator of his buildings against an otherwise neutral palette; the Fuksases' portraits emphasise their partnership, their male and female partnership, and by implication the avoidance of gender stereotyping in their work.

The hierarchical order of who counts in architecture is precisely drawn. The big guys are ever more powerful. But it is conceivable that the small guys can build up a following, with the favourite platform being the ubiquitous Instagram. Followers numbers provide one measure of their credibility. Foster's is pretty good at 242k. But MAD architects beat him with 321k. Zaha's continuing practice notches up 739k followers; not bad, but a mere shadow compared with other 'brands' like Gucci at 33.7M or Bella Hadid at 24.1M.

Of course there are multiple nuances of identity available to architects, especially in an age of gender dismorphia and inclusivity. They must position themselves on a variety of spectra that help reinforce not just how they look and what they produce: a barometer might read Individual/Collective, Artful/Technical, Cultural/Commercial. My own choice has been to the left on each one of these dials. But the more you (or your practice) swing to the right, the harder it seems to escape the blandification of the message. Unless, that is, you have achieved brand status.

**The Cool of School**

Meanwhile in the schools, where students are searching for ownership of their identities in lots of ways – professional and personal – the spread of profiles is as broad as society is large. But graduates are already aware of the profession being on the back foot and conformity soon steps in, not least because of the enormous cost of education.

Despite schools being just as business oriented as the practices, they are better at underlining the importance of ideas. Mediocrity does not have much of a market in education; schools vie for rankings and harness all means possible to attract the most talented students. Some students will have their eye on the reward of a healthy pay packet, but usually they choose the school most likely to nurture their own particular interests. They are faced with a difficult choice – becoming willing 'products' or fervent members of a style tribe: the shed-chitects, parametricists, contextualists or neo-postmodernists.

Nigel Coates,
Willendorf Hotel,
Voxtacity,
2017

The entire Voxtacity project makes use of found digital models of famous or archetypal artefacts. This famous prehistoric 'Venus' finds expression here as a multistorey building that encompasses all the curves and recesses of the original.

There is a whole side of architecture independent from practice. The visionaries fulfil that other trope, of being the dreamer architect whose ideas never see the light of day

The acute differences of approach in schools tend to get watered down as young designers pitch for work that must be produced on a tight budget, with hyper-rich clients thin on the ground, and the preferred style tends to be archetypal shed shapes made with the cheapest materials. Practice often undoes the coolness of school and has a levelling effect that fails to work even on Instagram. Every day on *Dezeen*, shed-shaped house extensions swish up the screen, at best promising their authors 15 seconds of fame. It will take an intriguing headline or a powerful image to make you 'read on'.

## A Broader Outlook

There is a whole side of architecture independent from practice. The visionaries fulfil that other trope, of being the dreamer architect whose ideas never see the light of day. In truth an architect's job is to be both dreamer and realist, out there in the field but with the head in the clouds. The ploughing of architectural ideas is vital for its culture to flourish, as it does consistently on the pages of this journal, with speculations on architecture that give context and voice to what was never intended to be built.

There are those practices that grasp the need to imagine and dream, yet test the dream and build it. Such are OMA, Hadid, Assemble, aLL DESIGN, BIG, Jean Nouvel, Fuksas. My list would also include practices that did not start out as architects, like Thomas Heatherwick and Olafur Eliasson, who incidentally *employ* architects. Eliasson has crossed increasingly from contemporary art environments into architecture, and is one of those people who can see how architecture can be functional and an art form.

The Italian designer-architect also comes to mind; more often a product designer than a maker of buildings, he or she acts as a producer, works closely with industry, and is more involved with product than the building architect. Take Piero Lissoni (Instagram 52.1k). His public profile equates to his personal signature, a vocabulary of soft simple shapes that are easy to like and comfortable to sit on. On the other hand, Kanye West, who has never been held back by a lack of ambition, believes he can bring a lot to the architects' table. He thinks of architecture as a 'product' like an album or a pair of sneakers, and as such better sustained by a brand of which he is the would-be mastermind.

Brands are prone to being bought and sold themselves, and that signals a further dilemma for the identity of the architect. What if a practice has sustained its profile, but lost its leader? Which goes to reinforce the more tangible identity of the smaller studio, and in particular those that cross into other fields and communicate through a broad palette of events and exhibitions as well as social media and real buildings. Stepping outside the frame can up the ante.

Nigel Coates,
David Hotel and Night World,
Voxtacity,
2017

Michelangelo's *David* provides a model that when turned through 90 degrees can be explored as a building complex with three interconnected levels. Avoiding traditional staircases, looping and ramped floors plot anatomic form that recalls musculature.

## Instant Architecture

Architects who merely promote their brand via an Instagram account are missing a whole universe of possibility. Communication needs backup from exhibitions, books, movies and, above all, experiences. Usually exhibitions of architecture are unmitigated disasters; instead of exploiting the fact that they show only representations of buildings, they sink to the evidence of full-sized details, models, drawings and photographs laid out on sample tables.

To show architecture successfully, and enrapture your audience, you need to make a narrative shift and enlist make-believe – as miniature, as movie, as constellation. Even Instagram can be made to exploit its own particular space. The grid format accumulates as a kind of architecture filled with the content of individual posts. As curator of your own account you can quickly follow those accounts that interest you, and hope they follow you. Insta has its own kind of democratic levelling; if you find an account to be too narcissistic (selfies), or boring (cats, food), or boastful (follower thresholds), you can cancel it. The potential for criticism resides in pithy text.

Which could be why in Adam Nathaniel Furman's world (pp 80–87) only the clever people win. But he, too, argues for the medium to be exploited for what it is. Ply it with provocation and you will get more back; treat it as a mood board saturated with your own projects and the chances are you will flatline.

If you are a more modest outfit, you need to define your USP in some other way, and like a successful political party searching for broad appeal, you need not be all things to all people. It goes to show that the last place you will truly understand the work of architects is by looking at their buildings. ⌂

# It goes to show that the last place you will truly understand the work of architects is by looking at their buildings

# CONTRIBUTORS

**Stephen Bayley** studied at Manchester University and the University of Liverpool School of Architecture. He worked first at the Open University and the University of Kent, where he established the history of design as a credible university subject. In the 1980s he led The Boilerhouse Project, an exhibition space devoted to design at the Victoria and Albert Museum in London. He was the Founding Director of London's Design Museum, and briefly Creative Director of the Millennium Dome. He is author of the book *Labour Camp: A Failure of Style Over Substance* (Batsford, 1998), a Chevalier de l'Ordre des Arts et des Lettres, International Fellow of the Royal Institute of British Architects (RIBA), Fellow of the University of Wales and Liverpool Institute of Performing Arts, and a Trustee of the Royal Fine Art Commission Trust.

**Thomas Bryans** is an architect and co-founder of the London-based architecture practice IF_DO. He leads the practice's research projects, and is passionate about a holistic approach to architecture: creating sustainable, beautiful and useful buildings that will be of long-term value to the communities and environment around them. He explored these ideas in his TEDx talk 'Architecture's Ripple Effect: Designing for Big Impact' in April 2017. He studied at both the University of Edinburgh and Harvard Graduate School of Design (GSD).

**Nigel Coates** trained at the Architectural Association (AA) in London, and founded the NATØ architecture group in the early 1980s. Since then he has consistently challenged the practice of architecture, overlapping it with fashion, design and the history of ideas. His inventive, artfully driven narratives have translated into many buildings, interiors and exhibitions around the world, particularly in Japan and the UK. His more experimental exhibition work includes *Mixtacity* at Tate Modern (2007) in London, and *Hypnerotosphere* at the 2008 Venice Architecture Biennale. As a designer of lighting and furniture he collaborates with many Italian companies including Alessi, GTV and Fornasetti. His publications include the semi-autobiographical *Guide to Ecstacity* (Laurence King, 2003) and *Narrative Architecture* (John Wiley & Sons, 2012). He is also a founding member of the London School of Architecture (LSA).

**Caroline Cole** read architecture at the University of Cambridge and during her professional life has worked both as a design consultant and as a client commissioning design professionals for the built environment. She is a Director of Colander Associates, and in this role has inspired many of the UK's most successful architectural practices to develop their businesses, and has worked alongside some of the most influential developers and building owners, helping to formulate their approach to architecture.

**Adam Nathaniel Furman** is a London-based designer whose practice ranges from architecture and interiors, to sculpture, installation, writing and product design. He co-runs the Saturated Space research group at the AA, and also pursued research through his three years running the Productive Exuberance studio at London's Central Saint Martins. He has worked at OMA Rotterdam, Ron Arad Associates, Farrells and Ash Sakula Architects, and has written for the *Architectural Review, RIBA Journal, Abitare, Icon* and *Apollo* magazines, among others. He is also co-author, with Sir Terry Farrell, of *Revisiting Postmodernism* (RIBA Publishing, 2017).

**Gabor Gallov** set up his own practice after working at notable offices such as Allies and Morrison and David Chipperfield Architects. He works mainly in central London on private houses, restaurants, shops and galleries, but has clients in Canada and the US. He teaches at Nottingham Trent University, and has been a visiting critic at Kingston University and the Royal College of Art (RCA) in London, and Cambridge University. He is a proponent of hand drawing as a primary tool throughout the design process and as an integral part of the education of an architect. His drawings are regularly published and have been exhibited at the RIBA.

**Jonathan Glancey** is a journalist, author and broadcaster. An Honorary Fellow of the RIBA, he writes for the *Daily Telegraph, BBC Culture, The Economist* and *CNN Style* among other publications and websites. He was Architecture and Design correspondent of the *Guardian* from 1997 to 2012, and Architecture and Design Editor of the *Independent* from 1989 to 1997. He is the author of *The Story of Architecture* (DK, 2003), *London: Bread and Circuses* (Verso, 2003), *Lost Buildings* (Goodman Books, 2015) and *Architecture: A Visual History* (DK, 2017), and co-author, with Norman Foster, of *Dymaxion Car – Buckminster Fuller* (Ivory Press, 2013).

**Justine Harvey** is based in Auckland, New Zealand, and writes about architecture and design. Until recently she was the editor of *Architecture New Zealand* and *Houses* magazines, and is currently the managing editor at ArchiPro, developing a new editorial platform within this fast-growing tech company. Prior to this she worked in the UK for 17 years in editorial, PR and communications for various publications and companies, including Richard Rogers Partnership (now RSH), Arup and ING Media.

**Owen Hopkins** is Senior Curator at Sir John Soane's Museum in London where he leads the exhibitions and learning teams. His interests revolve around the interactions between architecture, politics, technology and society. His most recent exhibitions include 'Eric Parry: Drawing' (2019), 'Code Builder' (with Mamou-Mani Architects), 'Out of Character' (with Studio MUTT) and 'The Return of the Past: Postmodernism in British Architecture' (all 2018). A frequent commentator on architecture in the press, he is the author of five books, including *Lost Futures* (2017) and *Mavericks: Breaking the Mould of British Architecture* (2016), both published by the Royal Academy of Arts, and *From the Shadows: The Architecture and Afterlife of Nicholas Hawksmoor* (Reaktion Books, 2015). He is also the guest-editor of *AD Architecture and Freedom* (May/June 2018).

**Roger Howie** studied at the University for the Creative Arts' School of Architecture, working in China and Southeast Asia before joining Zaha Hadid Architects in 2004 to lead the practice's media communications through the development of more than 150 built projects and product collections around the world, as well as retrospective exhibitions at the Guggenheim Museum in New York, State Hermitage Museum in St Petersburg, Design Museum in London and the Venice Architecture Biennale.

**Crispin Kelly** gained his first degree in Modern History from the University of Oxford. He founded the development and investment company Baylight Properties in 1982, went on to qualify as an architect, and has served as President of the AA. His charity, the Baylight Foundation, is based at Walmer Yard, four houses around a courtyard designed by Peter Salter, in London. The Foundation's aim is to deepen public understanding of experiencing architecture. His engagement with excellence and access in education continues as chair of both Open City and the LSA.

# THE IDENTITY OF
# THE ARCHITECT

**Jan Knikker** started his career as a journalist before shaping the public image of OMA for nearly a decade. As a partner at MVRDV, which he joined in 2008, he leads the contracts, business development and public relations efforts, forming a client-oriented, fast and strategic studio that includes a strong visualisation team and the practice's sustainability team. He has worked on many publications and exhibitions, and lectures internationally, at commercial and academic venues. He writes for various publications and is Deputy Editor of *Domus*. He is a member of the HNI Heritage Network, led the online design magazine *Dafne*, and from 2007 to 2011 was a member of the International Projects commission of the Netherlands Architecture Funds.

**Jay Merrick** was for several years the architecture critic for the *Independent* in London, and now writes on architecture and design for international publications including the *Architectural Review*, *Icon* and *Architects' Journal*. In his capacity as a consultant, he has written central texts for leading British and international architectural practices such as Grimshaws, Schmidt Hammer Lassen and Wilkinson Eyre. The subjects of his most recent monographs have been the Msheireb Museums in Doha, Eric Parry Architects, and the leading Mexican interior designer Gloria Cortina.

**Robin Monotti Graziadei** is a lecturer on cultural sustainability at the International Society of Biourbanism and a contributor to the *Journal of Biourbanism*. He graduated with an MA in the histories and theories of architecture from the AA, and later taught a postgraduate diploma unit at London Metropolitan University between 2001 and 2007, and a degree unit at the University of Greenwich in London. In 2007 he founded Robin Monotti Architects. Since 2016 he has been external examiner to the Moscow School of Architecture on behalf of London Met. In 2016 he set up Luminous Arts Productions to make feature films. He has also written an introduction to and translated Curzio Malaparte's *Woman Like Me* into English.

**Daria Pahhota** joined the Bjarke Ingels Group (BIG) in 2008. As Chief Communications Officer she oversees the studio's internal and external communication efforts, including media relations, branding and events. Over the past decade she has been presented with many diverse and challenging opportunities to articulate news about BIG's projects, express the company's vision and define its future. Through her support to various clients, constituents and internal partners and staff, the company has seen a tremendous growth in press and media outreach as well as a broader recognition and awareness of the company, brand, product and people.

**Juhani Pallasmaa** is an architect, professor emeritus and writer. He was previously Director of the Museum of Finnish Architecture, Professor and Dean of the Faculty of Architecture at Helsinki University of Technology, and has held several visiting professorships in the US. He has run workshops and lectures around the world, and was a member of the Pritzker Architecture Prize Jury from 2008 to 2014. He has published 60 books and 400 essays, and his writings have been translated into 35 languages. He is an honorary member of the Finnish Association of Architects (SAFA), American Institute of Architects (AIA) and the RIBA, and receiver of several national and international awards as well as five honorary doctorates.

**Vicky Richardson** is a writer and curator based in London. As Director of Architecture, Design and Fashion at the British Council (2010–16) she was Commissioner of the British Pavilion at the Venice Architecture Biennale. She lectures regularly on architecture and cities, and is a thesis supervisor for the MA in historical and sustainable architecture at New York University (London). She is former Editor of *Blueprint*, and Associate Director of the LSA. She advises a number of organisations on editorial and creative strategies, and is a member of the Advisory Panel of the V&A Dundee. In 2015 she was awarded an honorary fellowship of the RIBA.

**Ian Ritchie** is director of Ian Ritchie Architects, a Royal Academician, member of the Akademie der Künste, and a visiting professor at the University of Liverpool. He has chaired many international juries including the Stirling Prize, and has received two major international innovation awards, while his practice has won more than 100 national and international awards. He lectures internationally at conferences and universities. He has written several books, including poetry, and his art is in the collections of several international museums.

**Jenny E Sabin** is an architectural designer whose work is at the forefront of a new direction for 21st-century architectural practice – one that investigates the intersections of architecture and science and applies insights and theories from biology and mathematics to the design of material structures. She is the Arthur L and Isabel B Wiesenberger Professor in Architecture and Director of Graduate Studies in the Department of Architecture at Cornell University in Ithaca, New York where she established a new advanced research degree in Matter Design Computation. She is principal of Jenny Sabin Studio, an experimental architectural design studio based in Ithaca, and Director of the Sabin Lab at Cornell College of Architecture, Art, and Planning. She is co-author, with Peter Lloyd Jones, of *LabStudio: Design Research Between Architecture and Biology* (Routledge, 2017).

**Austin Williams** is an architect and course leader at Kingston University School of Art, and Honorary Research Fellow at the Xi'an Jiaotong-Liverpool **University** (XJTLU) in Suzhou, China. He is the director of the Future Cities Project, China correspondent for the *Architectural Review*, and author of *China's Urban Revolution: Understanding Chinese Eco-Cities* (Bloomsbury, 2017). The release of his latest book, *New Chinese Architecture: Twenty Women Building the Future* (Thames & Hudson, 2019) was accompanied by exhibitions in Shanghai and London. Together with Jiang Hao, his film *Edge Town/Che Fang* was shortlisted in the Arts and Humanites Research Council Awards 2018. He has written for a range of magazines including *Nature, Wired,* the *Times Literary Supplement, South China Morning Post, Metropolis* and *The Economist*. He is also the presenter of the Professional Practice Podcasts.

## What is Architectural Design?

Founded in 1930, *Architectural Design* (△) is an influential and prestigious publication. It combines the currency and topicality of a newsstand journal with the rigour and production qualities of a book. With an almost unrivalled reputation worldwide, it is consistently at the forefront of cultural thought and design.

Each title of △ is edited by an invited Guest-Editor, who is an international expert in the field. Renowned for being at the leading edge of design and new technologies, △ also covers themes as diverse as architectural history, the environment, interior design, landscape architecture and urban design.

Provocative and pioneering, △ inspires theoretical, creative and technological advances. It questions the outcome of technical innovations as well as the far-reaching social, cultural and environmental challenges that present themselves today.

For further information on △, subscriptions and purchasing single issues see:

**http://onlinelibrary.wiley.com/journal/10.1002/%28ISSN%291554-2769**

Volume 88  No 6
ISBN 978 1119 375951

Volume 89  No 1
ISBN 978 1119 453017

Volume 89  No 2
ISBN 978 1119 500346

Volume 89  No 3
ISBN 978 1119 546023

Volume 89  No 4
ISBN 978 1119 506850

Volume 89  No 5
ISBN 978 1119 546245